2/9/14

S0-AZO-744

Olga, You are my beautiful, faithful friend, God has migh... you... in my life, and I'm so thankful for you.

From Grief To Glory

"From The Fire Of Adversity
To The Fire Of His Love"

May His love continue to over flow in your life. His Bride, His passion, & His love are for you. Love you, Cathy

By

Cathy Coppola

From Grief To Glory

From the Fire Of Adversity To The Fire Of His Love

By

Cathy Coppola

Copyright @ 2014
All Rights Reserved
Printed in The United States of America

Published By:

ABM Publications
A division of Andrew Bills Ministries Inc.
PO Box 6811
Orange, CA 92863

www.abmpublications.com

ISBN: 978-1-931820-28-8

DEDICATION

I want to thank:

My loving husband, Phil

and my four beautiful children,

Valarie, Elise, David and Michael.

You are each a treasured gift of God to me.

My faithful friends: Diana, Stephanie, Sherri and Kristi, who labored with me in proofing and editing.

Each one of you are cherished in my heart.

My family and friends who prayed for me and never left me during my most difficult circumstances.

My Heavenly Father who has loved me, transformed me and called me His own.

TABLE OF CONTENTS

ACKNOWLEDGEMENTS

This book comes from the genuine prayer life of a faithful, dedicated woman of God. Cathy Coppola reminds me of the woman in Luke 18, her persistence in prayer and her love for God comes through in every page. As you read this book you will realize that these are not just lofty thoughts but a faith lived out, victories realized and a place of power and authority discovered. I know you will be thoroughly blessed and enriched as you read each page. Thank God for Cathy, she stands as a warrior and a reminder that our God is the God of resurrection and life. We now have the privilege of gleaning from wisdom gained through hours of grief and intense prayer. What an honor to have this to hold in our hands and hearts.

Christina Williams
Founder of Elevated to Excellence

Cathy has been a dear friend of mine since the early 90's. She is a devoted wife and mother and gifted teacher and leader in the body of Christ. God has blessed Cathy with the gift of faith and a fierce desire to see her family and all those she ministers to walking in the promises of God. Her example and teaching is desperately needed in the church today. Christians in the information age come to God's Word as consumers, cherry-picking Scripture for verses that support their opinions and beliefs. Forgotten is the fact that the Bible is holy and it is our precious sword in a rapidly decaying world. God has raised up Cathy Coppola to teach believers how to stand on God's Word in response to all of life's setbacks, disappointments, and losses. When you do, the healing, transforming power of God will bring renewal to your life and your world. My favorite aspect of this book are all the prayers that Cathy has composed – sentence by sentence- straight from the Bible. There is profound creative power in our thoughts and words. (2 Cor. 10:4-5) On your healing journey "From Grief to Glory" will show you how to declare and anchor yourself to God's truth. God's promises are what's real. All else are just circumstances that will change before your very eyes...if you put your trust in God and not in the way things appear. I'm so excited that God has led you to this book. Friend, you are about to be profoundly blessed!

Kristi Knudsen
Masters Degree in Education Leadership (2011)
Golden Gate Baptist Theological Seminary

From Grief to Glory is a deeply inspiring, and, at the same time, a very practical work. Cathy opens the depths of her heart to the reader, and *demonstrates* how to worship God through life's deep and diverse trials. Her devotion to God is palpable in her writing; her passion and zeal for His highest good is very real. She makes this path accessible to the reader with her thoughtful questions and challenges to which she asks the reader to respond. If you follow her leading, you can't fail to draw closer to the Father's Heart, and come out on the other side of your pain a stronger person.

Sherri Stewart
English Teacher

INTRODUCTION

This book chronicles my journey through loss, devastation and grief to a place of healing and intimacy with Jesus. Only the power of God could bring me from Grief to Glory. As I stood in the gap for my family, He changed me! He transformed me!

By the leading of the Holy Spirit, and obedience to the Lord, I wrote this book. The trials, tragedies, and traumas each one of us experience in life are meant to make us better, not bitter. We must learn how to walk through the heartache and get to the other side. On the other side of pain there is joy unspeakable, attainable for everyone.

If you have experienced any kind of lasting pain, loss, devastation, grief, even death, this book is for you. My desire is that you would read this book slowly and engage with the Holy Spirit, allowing Him to bring healing and transformation.

Regardless of why you find yourself in your current circumstances, whether they result from your own poor choices, from the choices of others or a little of both, with God there is always hope for a better tomorrow.

If I had to pinpoint one thing that drew me out of bitter waters to a place of heartfelt joy and security, it would be staying in the presence of Jesus. In His presence I have been transformed. He has encountered me many times and with each encounter He brought more healing to my heart and revelation to my spirit.

When I encountered devastation, I ran to Jesus and poured out my heart to Him in prayer. Then I stayed in His presence. Jesus has become more real to me than the air around me. I've been transformed in His presence.

If you want to see real change in your life you must make this an interactive journey with the Holy Spirit. My desire is that you read From Grief to Glory, allowing the Holy Spirit enough time to encounter you and transform you in His presence.

I suggest you journal, as you will find greater expression released from your heart to His as He reveals the truth of His heart to you.

This book is laid out in three sections. Each week, for eight weeks, you will find:

1. **A prayer.**

Read this prayer aloud daily. Prayer is the vehicle to cause change in any situation. Allow the Word of God to do for you what no man can do. The power of the spoken word is the power of change!

2. **Five devotionals, designed to help you interact with the Holy Spirit.**

Read the scriptures and meditate on them. They are the words of life. There are times reflective questions are asked. This is your opportunity to interact with the Holy Spirit and journal what the Lord reveals to you. Give Him the opportunity to direct you. It is important not to skip this step. We serve a God who wants to communicate with us and through us.

3. A message "From The Heart of The Father To His Beloved Bride."

This is written prophetically from the heart of the Father to you. The Father sees and knows what you've been through. He wants to blanket you with His love.

Allow the Holy Spirit to pour the love of the Father into you. His desire is for you to come to an understanding and a heartfelt experience of His great love for you.

Any italicized portion in this book reflects that the Lord is speaking.

Three keys for healing:

1. Daily, worship Jesus.
2. Daily, be still before Him in listening prayer.
3. Daily, interact with Him in prayer.

If you take this to heart and apply these three keys, I believe you will find that though your heart was once broken, you will become transformed and more alive in Him.

Make healing a priority. Give the Holy Spirit this eight-week time period to bring about the change only He can do. Allow the Father to speak to you through the Holy Spirit. Give Him permission to move through your mind, will and emotions. As you intentionally yield to Him, daily working through this book, He will take you from where you are in your spiritual journey and catapult you into heights you did not know existed.

Are you ready to begin your journey? Two months is not a very long time. I encourage you to begin today. I invite you to pray the prayer on the following page with me.

Prayer of Commitment

Father, in the name of Jesus, I come boldly, yet humbly, before Your throne of grace to obtain mercy and grace in time of need. Hebrew 4:16

I ask for Your Kingdom to come to my situation. Lord, You are my strength and my song, my rock and my redeemer, in You alone I trust. Psalm 18:2

I thank You for Your faithfulness in my life. You are the God who changes not, You are the same, yesterday, today and forever. Hebrew 13:8

My confidence remains completely in You. Thank You for being my sure foundation. Isaiah 33:6

Father, in the name of Jesus and by the power of the Holy Spirit, I commit this next eight weeks into your hands. I ask You to work an inner work in my heart. I am asking You to heal me and mold me into Your image. Remove from me any blinders or hardness of heart and show me the way of love. Heal me of my brokenness and bring me into a deeper walk with You.

I choose to yield to the Holy Spirit and walk in a manner that will bring You glory. I commit myself into Your hands, Jesus. I am Yours. I will do what You tell me to do. Cause my life to be pleasing unto You. Idesire to hear, when I stand before You one day, "Well done, good and faithful servant. You have been faithful with a few things; I will put you in charge of many things. Come and share in your Master's happiness!" Matthew 25:23.

Father, I call upon You now for Your wisdom and strength in the circumstances of life and for Your provision and rest. You are the God who abundantly supplies all my needs according to Your riches in glory. Philippians 4:19

Therefore, I rest in knowing all that I am in need of, I have, simply because You are a covenant-keeping God. Thank you Daddy for taking care of me, and all that concerns me today. Your word says, the ways of the Lord are perfect, the Word of the Lord is flawless. He is a shield for all who take refuge in Him. Psalm 18:30

Father thank You for arming me with strength and making my way perfect. Psalm 18:32 I know You will rescue me from my enemies. You will rescue me because You delight in me. 2 Samuel 22:20

Praise be to my Rock! Exalted be God my Savior. He is the God who avenges me, who subdues nations under me, who saves me from my enemies. You exalted me above my foes; from violent men You rescued me. Therefore I will praise You among the nations, O Lord; I will sing praises to Your name. You gave me great victories, showing unfailing kindness to Your anointed. 2 Samuel 22: 48-51

I lay all my concerns at Your feet, trusting also in You. I praise You for You counsel me, even at night my heart instructs me. Psalm 16:7

I have set the Lord always before me. Because He is at my right hand, I will not be shaken. Psalm 16:8

You have made known to me the paths of life, You will fill me with joy in Your presence. Psalm 16:11

I thank You and look expectantly for the beauty You will create from the ashes. I thank You for the oil of gladness You will bring instead of mourning and the garment of praise instead of a spirit of despair. Isaiah 61:3

I ask for the power of the Holy Spirit to transform me as I yield to You during this eight-week journey. Speak to me and cause me to hear You. I command any blinders to come off my eyes and heart and my for ears to be open to hearing You.

I bind any deaf and dumb spirit and command them in Jesus' name to be removed from me. I apply the blood of Jesus and completely surrender myself to my heavenly Father. I stand upon Your unchanging Word and I know that in due time, I will receive a double portion in this land and everlasting joy is mine in Jesus name. Isaiah 61:7

I bless You Lord and I love You. My mouth continues to give You praise in all of life's circumstances for You alone are good. I am Your bride, ready for You to create in me a heart after Yours. In Jesus' name I pray. Amen.

Conclusion

You made it! I am proud of you for staying the course and finishing this eight-week interactive journey. More importantly, God is pleased with you. This is just the beginning. All of life is a journey.

The catastrophe you walked through, the devastation that came upon you, the trials of life that you endured, all had the potential to either completely destroy you or to develop you into your God given destiny. Let me encourage you to keep going, pursuing healing as your Healer pursues you!

As we walk through the pain, consistently giving it to Jesus, He brings us out of life's most devastating circumstances into a land flowing with milk and honey. But you must allow Him to walk you through the process. Denial will only develop death in you.

The healing of emotions is a process for most people. Don't be impatient. Let God fully have His way with you. Beyond the pain is His glory. If you refuse to walk through the pain you will miss the glory. Deep calls unto deep. Allow Him to take you From Grief to Glory. There is a language of love layered in your journey, a healing balm to bring you to your fullness. Though this devotional is an eight-week journey, this is just the beginning. Continue to pursue Him and His presence daily.

The more you rest in Him, the faster and more thoroughly you will be healed. There is a depth of understanding that only comes to those that are willing to wait at His feet. Continue to bring your heartache to Him and let Him love you back to life. Give Him permission to encounter you. Then rest in His presence. He will transform you with His presence and bring healing and intimacy you never knew possible, simply because you gave Him time to do so. Be still before Him. Enjoy your journey; even in the midst of pain He will bring pleasure to your soul and life forevermore.

Jesus took me from a place of devastation, grief and desperation to a walk of intimacy with Him far beyond natural realms. He has completely transformed me in His presence. My heart that was once bound in pain now soars with delight, for I know His eyes are on me and His heart is for me. He has taken me into the heavenly spheres that this world knows not of.

There is so much more for you. Continue in your journey and do not settle for anything less. Let His presence speak over you. Let His love uproot the pain and transform your inner being into His glorious image. In His goodness He not only radically changed me, He rescued my family from the snares and entanglements of death. Only a God of glory could reach down and undo the devastation of sin. I give Him all the glory. He alone is faithful and He will do it for you as well. Each person's story is different, but God is always faithful and He deserves all the glory.

CATHY COPPOLA

Week One

GRIEF

1. Prayer of Dedication

2. A Mother's Lament

3. The Ark Of Safe Keeping

4. Abba Father Come

5. The Valley

6. Lose What You Love

7. The Heart of The Father to His Beloved Bride

Prayer of Dedication

2 Timothy 1:12
I know whom I have believed and am
persuaded that He is able to keep what I
have committed to Him until that day.

Father, I commit my children and grandchildren to You. I dedicate their spirit, soul and body to follow after Jesus. Father, cause them to know Your love and obediently walk in Your ways. I dedicate them to You to walk after the Spirit and not after the flesh. Galatians 5:16 Your Word says to commit your way to the Lord, trust also in Him and He shall bring it to pass. Psalm 37:5 Lord, I am trusting You to bring this to pass in their lives. I lay at Your altar my fears and disappointments I have had with them. I choose to trust You with their lives. I commit my own spirit into Your hands, knowing that You will direct my steps. Psalm 31:5 Lord, direct me when to speak into their lives and when I am to be silent and just pray. Because I have committed all things to You, I will keep praying and not lose heart. Luke 18:1

Your Word says that God is not a man, that He should lie nor a son of man, that He should change His mind. Does He speak and then not act? Does He promise and not fulfill? Numbers 28:19 Therefore, I am fully persuaded that what God has promised, He will also do. Romans 4:21 Father You said, My Word that goes forth from My mouth, shall not return to Me void, but will accomplish what I desire and achieve the purpose for which I sent it. Isaiah 55:11.

Therefore, I decree and declare the Word of the Lord over my family. My Spirit, who is on you, and My words that I have put in your mouth will not depart from your mouth, nor from the mouths of your children, nor from the mouths of your children's children from this time on and forever, says the Lord. Isaiah 59:20 &21

No matter how far away they are You said, Do not be afraid, for I am with you; I will bring your children from the east and gather you from the west. Isaiah 43:5 I choose to trust You and not be afraid, for You are a covenant keeping God. Children are a heritage from the Lord, and the fruit of the womb is a reward. Psalm 127:3

Your Word says, that You will go before me as a consuming fire. You will destroy my enemies and bring them down before me and I shall drive them out and destroy them quickly. Deuteronomy 9:3 I will drive out and destroy the enemy quickly by the blood of the Lamb and the word of my testimony. Revelation 12:11

I speak forth the living, powerful, Word of God. All my sons will be taught by the Lord and great will be my children's peace. Isaiah 54:13

I shall live by every Word that comes from the mouth of God. Matthew 4:4 I shall declare a thing and it will be established for me; so light will shine on my ways. Job 22:28

I thank You for all You have done and all You will do in the lives of my family members. In Jesus mighty name I pray.

A Mother's Lament

Psalm 147:11
The Lord takes pleasure in those who fear Him, in those who hope in His mercy.

Psalm 130:5
I wait for the Lord, my soul waits, and in His Word I do hope.

What do you do when catastrophe hits your family? What do you do when you stand in the gap and intercede for your loved ones; yet the devastation increases? During the low times in life the enemy will try to bombard you with all manner of blame, guilt and condemnation. If there is unconfessed sin, confess it to the Lord. Don't let the enemy oppress you with blame, guilt and condemnation. We must guard our hearts from his lies. The enemy of your soul would love to overwhelm you with shame. There is therefore now no condemnation to those who are in Christ Jesus, who do not walk according to the flesh, but according to the Spirit. Romans 8:1

We can all say, "I should have done this differently." The truth is, God is still in charge even in the midst our difficulties. He causes the sun to rise. He causes the winds to blow. Even if we had done everything exactly right in life, which is impossible, every one of us still has to deal with our humanity and our children are no different.

They must choose whom they will follow: the spirit or the flesh. Jesus is able to take our imperfections and make something beautiful from them. Our children need to make choices. Those choices cut like a knife to a mother's heart at times. I believe that is why we need each other, to rejoice with those who rejoice and mourn with those who mourn. For today it may be you going through a battle, tomorrow it may be another. Yet as we uphold each other's arms in the battle we will win the war. We must keep our eyes on Jesus. The pain of a broken heart is great and we must allow ourselves a season to grieve. With cries and shouts we mourn and agonize over the catastrophe that invaded our home and our hearts lament over the brokenness and loss all around us. Then when the mourning is over, we feel like we can breathe again. We sing again, we dream again. We will never be the same for our hearts have tasted death, and the agony of a bleeding heart remains. Yet, as we take pleasure in our God and hope in His mercy, we are enriched in every way. As we go through the fire and get to the other side, we bring the remembrance of the flames. That remembrance is what the Lord will use in us as we see others enter the flame of despair.

Sometimes the pain is so deep and everything seems to be a reminder of all that is lost. Allow yourself to grieve. For the day will come that you will need to be there as those you love pick up the broken pieces in their lives. They will need your tender love as they rummage through the rubble to try and find anything salvageable. In the mean time, in His mercy, He gives us time to heal. Keep taking all your pain to Him. He, of all people, knows full well our pain. For He suffered in every way, and relates to us in our time of need. Your pain may feel like death; like a grievous loss.

As with death one needs time to grieve. Give yourself time. Allow yourself to heal.

Remember it is a process. In the Old Testament, we read how David openly shared his emotions with the Lord. We must do the same. He was a man after God's own heart. God allowed him to grieve. He allowed him to express his pain.

Express your pain to the Lord for He already knows what you are going through. As you openly pour out your heart to God, He will begin His work of bringing peace, healing and hope. Allow yourself to be broken and real before Him. He will wipe away your tears and hold them in a bottle. All your prayers will be like incense before Him rising up to His throne. He hears and will respond. Wait for the Lord, and hope in His word. Moment by moment allow your broken heart to come before Him.

He alone can heal, He alone can restore.

Reflection:

Don't waste your pain. Allow Him to heal you. Come before Him and if your heart is bound up with emotions and you do not know how to express them, ask the Holy Spirit to help you to feel what He wants you to feel at this moment in time. Ask Him to pray through you. Lay at His feet everything He shows you that you were never meant to carry. You were not meant to carry the grief from your catastrophe. Give it to Jesus. He is waiting.

The Ark of Safe Keeping

Genesis 7:17 & 20
For forty days the flood kept coming on the earth,
and as the waters increased they lifted the ark high
aabove earth. The waters rose and covered the
mountains to a depth of more than twenty feet.

The flood was a flood of judgment, but the righteous were lifted up. Noah and his family were lifted up and spared the judgment of death. How many times have you felt the pain of someone's poor decisions? How many times have you felt you were negatively affected by another's actions?

I believe Noah could have related, yet he remained faithful to God. In doing so, his circumstances were lifted up. If we remain faithful even when we are tempted to blame others for the circumstances we find ourselves in, the Lord will lift us up.

Noah was lifted up, Gen. 7:20 states; the waters covered the mountains to a depth of over twenty feet! The Lord will lift you high above your circumstances, if you don't give in to the downpour of negativity and persecution you may be enduring.

What mountain stands in your path? What obstacles are you facing? The Lord wants to bury those mountains in your life that keep you from the fullness in your relationship with Christ. Not just cover them, but bury them 20 feet deep! The waters of judgment for some were the waters of salvation for Noah. The same is true for us.

CATHY COPPOLA

One person's judgment can be your release, if you remain faithful to the Lord in your trial.

Do not despise the negative circumstances in your life. The things that cause us to complain are the things He wants us to bring to Him and lay at His feet. Cry out to the Lord for your deliverance; cry out to Him to remove the mountains in your life.

Sometimes there is a waiting process. Remember, even Noah had to wait for the waters to recede. The promise comes to those who are patient. Noah was blessed for his obedience and God made a covenant with him. In the midst of any storm keep your eyes on the promise, not the problem. The waters will recede and you will be lifted up.

Father, I give You my hopes, dreams and disappointments. I give You my mistakes, my judgments and my ways that do not please You. I give You my heart. Take my life; use me for Your purposes. Cause me to see You in every situation. Cause me to be emptied of myself and filled with Your Spirit every day.

Here I am Lord. Would You take this mess and make something beautiful of it? Father, I ask that You would send the wind of Your Spirit on the things I cannot change. Would You cause the torrents of life to recede and send the waters of liberation? Would You give me the grace to handle what I must go through, and strength for the things I must stand against?

Father, remember me as You remembered Noah. Speak, for I am listening. I will wait for Your voice. Where You lead, I will follow. I am Your beloved. Amen

Reflection:

In your greatest trial, how has the Father comforted your heart? How has He become more real to you?

Abba Father Come

Romans 8:15
You did not receive the spirit of bondage
again to fear, but you received the
Spirit of adoption by whom we cry out,
"Abba, Father."

In desperation we cry out, "Father come." In agony we lay there as in a sea of catastrophic events. "Father, what has happened? How did we get here? Surely You have a plan." We cry out for His grace to lift us from the mire. Movement all around us; yet it's the stillness of death we feel. Even so, even in our death, we have hope. He is our hope; He is becoming more and more real to us. For we have received the Spirit of adoption and our spirits cry out to Him. Heaven hears the silent cry. Heaven knows your deepest agony. Heaven responds to rescue you.

God of heaven and earth, Father, Son and Holy Spirit, we call unto You. We cry out "Abba Father, come." I am Yours and You are mine. For You rescued me from the grave. Out of the deepest, waterless pit you redeemed me because I am your beloved.

Remember, if we want to share in His inheritance, we must also share in His sufferings. Tasting of His glory, His deep intimacy, and the beauty realm of God is free, yet costly, difficult, yet worth it all. Abandon all for the sake of the Gospel. He wants you to come freely. Yet to truly come into His richest inheritance, you must surrender all. You must die to self and count the cost to receive the richest of fare from His heart of love.

Lord, whom have I but You? You pour out Your Spirit and lavish me with Your treasures; the treasure of knowing that I am Yours and You are mine. I am Your bride. You are my Husband. Easily spoken yet costly to live out. You spoke to me, "One life for the life of many." Yes Lord, I will answer the call, "One life for the life of many." I surrender all to You. Have Your way in my life. I am utterly abandoned to You, totally surrendered to You. You have wrapped Your arms of love around me. You have changed me on the inside. Though my circumstances lay in shambles, I leap for joy at the sound of Your name.

Be still and know that I am God. In pain you find passion; His passion. Pain is the catalyst to breaking down the barriers; barriers that keep you from Him. Come to Me all you who are weary and burdened, and I will give you rest. Matt. 11:28 I will break the gates of bronze, and cut the bars of iron in two. Ps. 107:16 As for you also, because of the blood of your covenant, I will set your prisoners free from the waterless pit. Zechariah 9:11

Reflection:

What great losses have you suffered during your fiery trial? Give your brokenness to the Lord and let Him comfort you. There is beauty in loss that will be found in no other way. The Heavenly King has adopted you. Let Him lavish His love on you and secure your wounded heart. Be still before Him now and give Him time to heal your brokenness.

The Valley

Psalm 23:4
Yea, though I walk through the valley of the shadow of death, I will fear no evil; for You are with me; Your rod and Your staff, they comfort me.

The valley is all about death, our death. Learn to die quickly in the valley. Learn to say to the Lord, "I surrender, my will, my desire, and my dreams. I surrender and commit my life to You. I want to be set free from any bondage that I carry."

Lord, in the valley when it feels like all is being stripped away, I stand still and let You kill everything in me that does not bring You glory. I surrender my right to be right even if I was right. I surrender my heart's desire to You and commit to carrying Your heart within me for every situation. Lord, burn up everything within me that is of the flesh, everything within me that is unsanctified. Conform me to Your image. I will follow You no matter what. I will serve You no matter what. I will cling to You no matter what, for I am Yours.

Do not despise your valley. Your valley is meant to prepare you for great exploits. It is meant to burn away the dross and make you strong, stronger than ever.

In your valley, God desires for you to learn how to:

• Lean and cling to the Spirit of God.
• Die and surrender all things to Him.
• Pray with authority.
• Rejoice in all things.

Your time in the valley is a time of refining, strengthening and preparing you for your victory, which lies ahead.

Reflection:

Are you ready to surrender all? Tell Him in your own words to "kill this flesh." Then be ready. He will take you seriously. Life may get worse before it gets better, but He will honor your heart of abandonment to Him. In the end, only what we do for Christ will matter. Live sold out for Him. What can man do to you? You belong to Him.

Lose What You Love

John 12:23-29

Jesus replied, "The hour has come for the Son of Man to be glorified. Very truly I tell you, unless a kernel of wheat falls to the ground and dies, it remains only a single seed. But if it dies, it produces many seeds. Anyone who loves their life will lose it, while anyone who hates their life in this world will keep it for eternal life. Whoever serves me must follow me; and where I am, my servant also will be. My Father will honor the one who serves me. "My soul is troubled, and what shall I say? 'Father, save me from this hour'? No, it was for this very reason I came to this hour. Father, glorify Your name!" Then a voice came from heaven, "I have glorified it, and will glorify it again." The crowd heard it said it sounded like thunder; others said an angel had spoken to Him.

Jesus came to the hour where His heart was troubled, yet He knew that He would willingly be lifted up and draw all men to Himself. Before He was glorified He had to suffer and die. In His death He produced life; multiplication of life. A kernel of wheat must fall to the ground and die, for in dying many seeds are produced. Jesus had to die to produce many offspring.

If you serve Christ you must follow His ways. God will honor the one who serves Him. As Jesus died to produce much, you too will have to die to produce much and glorify the Father. What must die in your life in order for the Father to be glorified; a dream, a desire, a relationship? What must you let go of in order to allow God's multiplication processto operate in your life? Is there a loved one bent on going their own way? You must completely release them to the Lord. Though it may feel like death, death brings life to those who willingly die. We must willingly give to Jesus any area of fear this may bring up. Will you trust Jesus with your hopes, dreams, fears and disappointments?

Remember, in dying you live, in living you die. Give Him your pain and trust Him to bring life out of what seems dead. Ask Him to revive in you His dreams for you. He who loves his life will lose it, and he who hates his life in this world will keep it for eternal life. John 12:25

In other words, anyone who willingly surrenders their personal desires to the Lord because they desire to be in complete surrender to Him will gain, preserve and protect their life for eternity. Ask Him to strengthen you and guide you as you surrender to Him the things that need to die in your life. Put them on the altar and allow them to die. Release your control of the situation. Let the pain and brokenness of your heart's desire go at His altar. Surrender your fragmented hopes, broken dreams, and lost desires.

Let the seed fall to the ground. Remember, unless a kernel of wheat falls to the ground and dies, it remains only a single seed. But if it dies, it produces many seeds. Anyone who loves their life will lose it, while anyone who hates their life in this world will keep it for eternal life. John 12:24 & 25. Cast your bread upon the waters for after many days you will find it again. Ecclesiastes 11:1

Father, search my heart and show me what must die. What is holding me back from completely releasing control to You? What is causing me to remain in fear? I know You honor faith, and fear will keep me in bondage.

Show me what must die in my life in order to produce much good fruit. I willingly release it to You and let You direct my life. I am Yours and You are mine. You are my Father, and I choose to glorify Your name.

Reflection:

Communication is the key to relationships. Are you communicating with the Lord? Are you asking Him detailed questions or are you running to others with your questions? Be still before Him and ask Him what must die in your life. Then journal what He reveals to you. Make a commitment that you will yield your heart and your mind to Him today.

The Heart of The Father to His Beloved Bride

Silent Cries

My beloved, I hear the silent cries, I see the hidden tears, I feel your broken and contrite heart; these I will not despise. The agony you feel in your bones, the gasp of your spirit which longs for air, these will pass. Be still, even the numbness will melt away; the dreariness will subside. The sun will shine again. The first day of spring shall blow in. The wind of the Spirit, the very breath of God shall strengthen you again.

My daughter, though the stench of death permeates the air all around you, I will carry you. You have found delight in My heart. Our hearts have become one and I will carry you through this. I will cause you to soar over the heights of your catastrophe. You will see from above down to the circumstances. You will have my perspective, heavenly eyes to see, to really see. This attack against your family will cease, but I must use you to go through this battle and fight. Stay in My presence. The battle is too strong to attempt without the constant presence of My wind beneath you. You are My chosen one. I will use the sword I put in your hand to fight this battle and win. Stay strong my daughter.

Remember, I am with you and am carrying you. I must use you to defeat this massive attack and free your family. In Me, you will have victory for your loved ones, and in Me, you will soar to new heights. The sacrifices of God are a broken spirit, a broken and contrite heart; These, O God, You will not despise.
Psalm 51:17

CATHY COPPOLA

Week Two

BROKEN

1. Prayer To Draw Our Loved Ones Heart To God

2. Choose Joy

3. I Will Not Move Without Your Spirit

4. In Your Agony Choose to Bless Him

5. Kept My Feet From Slipping

6. Bitter Waters Sweet

7. I Will Not Allow The Enemy To Destroy You

Prayer To Draw Our Loved Ones Heart To God

Father, we lift up our children and grandchildren to You. We ask You to watch over them and surround them with Your presence. Draw them to Your heart. Cause them to hunger and thirst after You. Lord, give them the grace to forgive whomever they need to forgive. Soften their hearts that they would see their need for forgiveness.

Father, create in them a pure heart and renew a steadfast spirit within them. Psalm 51:10. Lord, remove the wicked one from among them. Cause them to be attracted to, and to attract, godly friends and spouses. Work in them to both to will and to do according to Your good purposes. Philippians 2:13

Strengthen them with might through the Spirit of God in their inner man. Ephesians 3:16. Cause Christ to dwell in their hearts through faith. Ephesians 3:17. Cause them to be rooted and grounded in love, that they would know the love of Christ, which passes all knowledge. Ephesians 3:17-19. Fill them with the goodness of knowing You. Lord, keep them from all harm, and watch over their life. Psalm 121:7

Watch their coming and their going both now and forever more. Psalm 121:8. Give them an undivided heart that they would fear Your Name. Psalm 86:11 Pour Your Spirit on them. Acts 2:17. Contend with those who contend with them and save our children. Isaiah 49:25. Rescue them from the fowler's snare; from their own ignorance and immaturity. Psalm 91:3. Lead and guide our children and grandchildren with Your peace. Cause them to want to go to church and be involved with small groups. Give them godly friends. Remove any lure or enticement from ungodliness and develop in them a desire for godliness.

Father, let them not waste their years in rebellion. Draw their hearts to You and work in them a heart after You. For those that do not know You as their Savior, save their souls. Cause them to cry out to You and bring godly people into their lives that will lead them to Christ and good fellowship. Encounter them this week with Your love. Set up divine appointments and let them know that You are with them. Fill them with Your love and Your healing. Lead them to churches where they will be able to grow and become established. Give them a sense of belonging to the family of God and their own families.

Father, we ask for wisdom and discernment as we parent our children. Lead us by Your Spirit of truth. John 16:13 Show us what to do and what to say to them. Cause them to have unity in their sibling relationships and their relationships with their parents. Break off any spirit of division and strife from our families. Release Your peace in our homes. Fill us with the power of Your Spirit. We release each and every one of them into Your hands. We trust You with them and we know that what You have begun You will be faithful to complete. Philippians 1:6

We love You and ask for a greater increase of Your presence in our homes. We bless You Lord. You are faithful.

Our hope and confidence is in You alone. In Jesus name we pray. Amen.

Choose Joy

Psalm 27:13
I would have lost heart unless I had believed,
that I would see the goodness of
the Lord in the land of the living.

Yea, though I walk through the valley of the shadow of death, I will choose joy. Though the wind and waves assail me and long I stand in battle, I will choose joy. I will choose thanksgiving. When strength becomes weakness and contentment despair; when heaviness surrounds you and fear is beside you; look up, for your redemption draws nigh. Choose joy and chose life.

Choosing joy is choosing Jesus; not because circumstances are good, but because of a quiet resolve, an inner commitment in your heart. In Him we find life. In Him we find strength. In Him we find treasures, yes, even treasures out of our darkness. It's found in Him. Choose joy, choose Jesus and live. Don't let your circumstances dictate your life. You will have to choose joy during your lowest of lows. It won't be done for you. It is required of you. Yes, required. For Jesus has chosen joy, He chose death so you could live. He chose rejection so that you would be accepted. He chose utter despair and loss of every kind, so you could find life. Choose joy, choose Jesus and live.

You may ask, when did He choose death? When did He choose rejection? When did He choose despair and loss of every kind? He chose these before the creation of time. The cross was chosen before time began. Jesus went to the cross and all our pain, sorrows, and disappointments were nailed to Him. Willingly, He went for you and for me.

His love looked across the span of time and chose you before you even existed. Therefore, In Him we can choose to draw upon His strength and choose joy even when we are not joyful.

When you choose joy, you are choosing His strength for your weakness, His life for your death. What is dead or seems dead in your life? Choose joy, choose Jesus and live. For in choosing Him you will find strength you never knew existed. That strength is His strength working in you. He gives strength to the weary and increases the power of the weak. Isaiah 40:29

When you choose joy, you find peace and contentment working in you; His peace, in the midst of every storm. The peace of God, which transcends all understanding, will guard your heart and your mind in Christ Jesus. Philippians 4:7.   My yoke is easy and my burden is light. Matthew 11:30.   When you choose joy, you find the weight of heaviness lifted, because His yoke is easy and His burden is light.

He is a rewarder of those who diligently seek Him. Hebrews 11:6b. He already paid the price. Wait on the Lord; be of good courage, and He shall strengthen your heart. Wait, I say, on the Lord. Psalm 27:14.   Do not lose heart. Believe Him, and you will see beauty come from your ashes. But you must choose joy. He won't do it for you, for He already has done all He could do. He did for us what we could not do for ourselves; so that through Him we would be able to do all that was required of us. Choose Jesus, choose joy and live. Watch Him bring redemption, abundance, and fruitfulness through you.

Father, today I choose joy. Some days I choose joy and everything around me is good and I am thriving. Other days it is not so. On those harder days remind me to choose joy. When the world is caving in on me and hopelessness and despair is all I feel, on those days I resolve to choose You. I resolve to choose Jesus the one who paid it all. I choose as an act of my will to say, "Thank you Lord"; when I am abased and when I am abounding; when there is much or when there is little. I choose to be thankful when things are going for well me and when they are not. I will not lose heart because I choose to believe that I will see the goodness of the Lord in my life; not just on good days but on the hard days too.

I will choose joy, I will choose Jesus, and I will live. I will watch You turn it all around. For in You I find peace and joy. In You I find contentment and purpose. In you I find life, the greatest gift of all: the gift of Your love for me. It is all found in You and You are in me; so it is found in me. It all abides in me today. So I choose to believe that since the greater one lives in me, I already have all I need for life and godliness. Jesus, I choose You. I choose joy for You have made my joy complete.

Reflection:

In what ways have you chosen joy in the midst of difficult circumstances? How has that changed your perspective?

I Will Not Move Without Your Spirit

Psalm 62: 1-6
Truly my soul silently waits for God; from Him comes my
salvation. He only is my rock and my salvation; He is my
defense; I shall not be greatly moved. How long will you
attack a man? You shall be slain, all of you, like a leaning
wall and a tottering fence. They only consult to cast him
down from his high position; they delight in lies; they
bless with their mouth, but they curse inwardly. My soul,
wait silently for God alone, for my expectation is from
Him. He only is my rock and my salvation; He is my
defense; I shall not be moved.

Dearly beloved of God, when you are surrounded by brokenness and loss of every kind and you find yourself in utter despair, don't run, don't hide. Sit before the Father. Let Him heal you. Let Him love you back to life. When your heart has been pierced by swords laced with venom; when all you feel is the pain of your shattered heart; don't turn to others, turn to Jesus. Sit. Lie prostrate before Him.

Throw yourself on the mercy of God to heal you. He is the greatest physician of all. He will heal you and give you life again. Do not move from His presence until His hand has blanketed your wounded heart. For He alone is Your God. He alone can carry you through the fiercest of storms and set you high above your enemies.

My soul longs for You my Lord, my all encompassing one. I wait in the stillness of Your presence, captivated by Your love. There is stillness in the midst of swirling; emotions and thought's racing, then becoming still. Yet, through it all, my spirit is unmoved. I remain steadfast,

set securely on You. I am pressing in, and pressing on. For I have tasted and I know Your love is better than life. Your love is all I need. Come, presence of God, and fill me anew. I will not move without Your Spirit. Fill me anew for You are all I long for, sweet presence of God. In You I move and have my being. For You I will wait. I long for You. My heart thirsts for You. Early in the morning I shall seek You. Take not Your presence from me.

Reflection:

Jesus wants to take your pain and bring forth something beautiful. Sit before Him and ask Him to walk you through your pain and bring His healing. Journal what He shows you.

In Your Agony Choose to Bless Him

Isaiah 58:12-14
Those from among you
Shall build the old waste places;
You shall raise up the foundations of many generations;
And you shall be called the Repairer of the Breach,
The Restorer of Streets to Dwell In.
Father, shattered pieces lay all around, broken and
scattered; yet my eyes are on You, Oh Most Holy One,
lover of my soul! My deepest anguish turns to
shouts of exhilaration, shouts of victory, shouts of praise.
You have torn me, but you will heal me. You are holy.
You are my Deliverer, the Repairer of the Broken Walls,
the Restorer of Streets with Dwellings.

Beloved, are there old waste places in your life lying in
ruins? Has a plague of locusts devoured promises that
were in the making? Rise up, even in your brokenness and
look to the barrenness all around. Declare to the
devastation, "The foundations of many generations will be
raised up!" Don't allow despair to remain and unfulfilled
dreams to lie in shambles. Beloved, You shall raise up the
foundations! You shall be called the repairer of the breach
and restorer of streets to dwell in. What in your life needs
repairing? What needs restoring? Don't allow the crisis
you face to keep you stuck in your situation. Rise up and
fight with the strong arm of the Lord. He is your strength
and your shield. Fight, beloved of God! Reclaim what is
yours!

I called on the Lord and He answered me. He has filled me
with His joy. He has caused me to ride on the heights of
the land to feast on my inheritance. In brokenness I

choose to rejoice. Soul, bless Him who rides on the clouds of creation. I looked at the devastation all around me and with the shout of faith, reclaimed what had been utterly destroyed and stolen from me. In your brokenness and devastation, rise up and declare that He alone is good.

Choose to bless Him in your agony and distress. For in doing so, your offering will be a sweet incense to the King; sacrificially offered with each expression of costly worship. He will turn your anguish into elation for Him.

Reflection:

Make a list of what the enemy has stolen from you. Make specific declarations that what has been stolen will be retrieved. Declare His word over what has been lost and stand, mighty one of God. Stand for yourself and your loved ones.

Kept My Feet From Slipping

Psalm 66:8-14
Praise our God, all people, let the sound of His praise be heard; He has preserved our lives and kept our feet from slipping. For You, God, tested us; You refined us like silver. You brought us into prison and laid burdens on our backs. You let people ride over our heads; we went through fire and water, but You brought us to a place of abundance. I will come to Your temple with burnt offerings and fulfill my vows to You, vows my lips promised and my mouth spoke when I was in trouble.

Father, I praise You for You have kept my feet from slipping. You have been my sure foundation. When all others failed me and I was found in the barren winter alone, You reached down from Your sanctuary above and carried me through. Though You tested me and refined me as silver and though it felt like I was in a prison with burdens on my back, Your loving arms sustained me and carried me through.

You allowed waves of grave adversity to come against me and the waters almost drowned me. I felt the flames of affliction burn me. Yet Your unfailing love sustained me. Your presence melted away the burden and pain of adversity. Then in triumph You rode across the skies and brought me to a place of abundance. With burnt offerings I come to Your temple and fulfill my vows to you. Vows my lips promised and my mouth spoke when I was in trouble. "Lord my life is Yours. Do unto me as You wish. May my life be a sweet fragrance burning unto You Lord. Use me for Your glory. If my life is required, my life will be given. For You said Lord, 'One life for the life of many.'

Yes Lord, no matter what, I will serve You. May my life be like a sweet fragrance continually rising before You."

Reflection:

What vows have you made to Him? Have you fulfilled your vows? What is He asking of you right now? Surrender both your pain and your pleasure, for this life has nothing for you. Write your heart's response. Ask Him, "Lord, what vow have I made that I have not kept?" "What do You desire I let go of?"

Be obedient to what He shows you. You will not regret it.

Bitter Waters Sweet

Matthew 5:4
Blessed are those who mourn,
for they shall be comforted.

Oh God, my God, I rest in Your presence, resting in Your love. For You alone my heart sing for You alone my heart beats. Your love is a mighty rushing river; mighty and rushing indeed.

Oh Lord, when the waters of life become embittered and when the tragedies of life become too painful to bear, to You I cry out.

In desperation of soul, I cry out to the Lord, the faithful One. Lord, it's Your cross that makes the bitter waters sweet. I cry out for Your hand, Lord.

Make the bitter waters sweet.

Reflection:

When you look to eternity, can you see the current pain, grief and struggle dissipate into His arms of love? Ask Him to take the sting, the bitter pain away.

Ask Him to give you a perspective of eternity in light of your pain and to exchange your pain for His constant and steady love.

The Heart of the Father To His Beloved Bride

I Will Not Allow The Enemy To Destroy You

2 Thessalonians 3:3 & 5
The Lord is faithful; He will strengthen and protect you from the evil one. May the Lord direct your heart into God's love and Christ's perseverance.

My beloved, I am the Lord Your God. I am faithful to carry out what I have revealed to you. The downpour of destruction will not overtake you. Call out to Me, for I will strengthen you and cause you to rise up above the devastation marked out against you.

Be still and know that I am God. Wait in My presence. Do not falter; do not grow weary. The enemy's plan is to exhaust you so he can wipe you out, because you are My beloved, and you yield to Me. I will not allow him to destroy you.

I will protect you from his master plan to completely derail you. I am your strong tower, the righteous run to Me and they are safe. I will protect you from the evil one. Keep your heart focused on Me, on My love and Christ's perseverance.

Week Three

SURRENDER

Prayer for Wisdom, Revelation and Understanding

Ephesians 1:16-23

Father, I do not cease to give thanks to You, the God of our Lord Jesus Christ, the Father of glory. I ask You to give us the spirit of wisdom and revelation. Father, give us the spirit of wisdom; practical wisdom, and sound judgment for our daily lives. Cultivate our minds and enlighten our understanding. Along with practical wisdom, would You give us divine wisdom, knowledge and insight from Your word, that we would truly know You. Father, give us the spirit of revelation; bring to light, reveal and uncover any ways of darkness we may be walking in. Cause us to see the vanity of it. Remove the veil of ignorance and darkness by the entrance of Your word that we would fully discern and fully know the truth.

Father, I ask that the eyes of our understanding be enlightened; that we may know what is the hope of Your calling, what are the riches of the glory of our inheritance, and what is the exceeding greatness of Your power toward us who believe. Father, I pray that our mind, the ways of thinking and feeling would be enlightened, lit up and made clear according to Your word. Father, enlighten us with spiritual knowledge and understanding according to Your great power. Father, according to Your mighty power which You worked in Christ when You raised Jesus from the dead and seated Him at God's right hand in the heavenly places, far above all principality, power, might and dominion, raise us high above the power of darkness and deception, and bring us into Your wonderful light.

Your name is above every name that is named, not only in this age but also in that which is to come. You put all things under Jesus' feet, and gave Him to be head over all things to the church, which is the body of Christ.

Father, You said, I shall declare a thing and it shall be established for me. Job 22:28 You said the entrance of Your word gives light, it gives understanding to the simple. Ps. 119:130 Therefore, I declare that we walk in the spirit of wisdom and revelation in the knowledge of Jesus Christ and the eyes of our understanding are enlightened to fully know You, love You and serve You Lord. I pray all this in the name of Jesus. Amen.

I Died; Now Christ

Lamentations 3:22
Because of the Lord's great love we are not consumed, for his compassions never fail.

The refining fire of life's adversity has completely remolded me and reshaped me. I can truly say, "Death has no mastery over me, death has no sting. I died a thousand deaths, now I live securely in Christ." I can relate to Paul who wrote, "For me to die is gain, to live is Christ." I live for one sole purpose, to do the will of my Father.

When circumstances force you into cruel, harsh, devastating situations; when you're left standing face to face with gripping fear, tormenting thoughts and circumstances beyond your control, surrender. Fall on your face and cry out for mercy. When darkness is all around you and there is no glimmer of hope, be still and know that He is God. When you think you've gone as far as you can go, yet more is still required of you; when the enemy relentlessly pursues you, don't leave your post. Stand strong in the Lord. Even if you don't think you have anything left in you, do it anyway. You cannot leave your post. You cannot walk away from your assignment, for in your weakness He is strong. Surrender all for the sake of the cross. Learn to die daily. Die to your greatest fears. Don't let them rule your life.

Like Paul, we too must be able to say, "I have died, now I live in Christ." What can man do to me? Nothing, because when you die, you gain. I have gained all and my faith is unshakable. There is no mountain too high;

there is no valley too low that I cannot cross. For when you die, you live.

I live in Christ, like never before. The threat of death has lost its power. Fear no longer has mastery over me. I've been through the fires of unshakable death; stripped of all that was dear to my heart. I rose from the ashes; yet not I but Christ in me rises. I am full of faith, for He has given me the gift of faith. When you die, you truly live. I live surrendered to Christ therefore I gain all.

Fear not, for I am with you; be not dismayed, for I am your God. I will strengthen you, yes, I will help you, I will uphold you with My righteous right hand. Isaiah 41:10

Reflection:

If you let Him, He will gird you up and uphold you in every trial of life. How have you seen His faithfulness in your life? In what way has your trust in Him grown?

No Matter What

Psalm 51:17
The sacrifices of God are a broken spirit; a broken and
contrite heart, O God, You will not despise.

We must resolve in our hearts that we will trust Him no matter what happens in life, even if all is required of us. If everyone turns against you and you find yourself standing alone; whether you are in good health or not; whether you are prospering or not; or whether you are experiencing emotional pain, we must resolve in our hearts that we will serve Him and love Him with all our heart, no matter what the cost.

He is looking for those who are fully committed to Him, who will not bow their hearts to another. Those who have committed in their hearts that whatever comes their way will not move them from their commitment to the One they love. He is worth it all; all pain, all trials, all persecution. He is worthy! What costs have been asked of you? Never will you out give the King. He has paid the ultimate price; the ultimate sacrifice has been paid.

Lord, I will not offer unto You that which costs me nothing. Shatter all of the pentup places of my heart. Tear down every wall of resistance. I will give You

the sacrifice of praise. I will let my tears flow before you like incense, rising up before you like a sweet sacrifice. Surely, you are closer than my mother or father. You are my Creator, my Husband, and my Friend. When all else fails me, when everyone has abandoned me and all

things are required of me, still I will praise you. Still I will choose you. Still I will love you, no matter what. For You alone have taken my fearful heart and secured it with Your love.

Lord, I know that:
- You are for me.
- You are my rescuer.
- Though the righteous falls seven times, seven times he rises again.
- You require obedience, not sacrifice.
- You will never forsake me in my weakness.
- You will lift me up on eagle's wings.
- Your mercies are new every day and Your love is unending.
- You hold my heart in the palm of Your hands.
- I am Your forever lover.
- You will protect me from the venom that is leashed upon me.
- You surround me as with a shield.
- You will lift me from this mire and make me new.

Lord, a sacrifice of brokenness is what I offer unto You. Whatever is required of me, I give to You. Break me so that You can mold me into Your image, for I have resolved to give You glory. How can my brokenness give You the most glory? Show me Lord.

Reflection:

We must be broken before Him before we can live. Brokenness unto Him is His desire. Are you willing to let go of all you are hanging on to and completely surrender all to Him? Are you willing to tell Him to break off all that keeps you from His love? He will take you seriously. Remember the pain will last for a moment, but the pleasure forevermore.

Surrender Both Pain and Pleasure

2 Samuel 24:24
David said, "I will surely buy it from you for a price; nor
will I offer burnt offerings to the Lord my God with that
which costs me nothing." So David bought the threshing
floor and the oxen for fifty shekels of silver.

I will not offer to God that which costs me nothing. With joy and sorrow I step forward, knowing that my hope, my life, and my very breath lies with my Savior, my King.

Lord, what can I give to You, what can I say to You? You are my beautiful King. My soul delights in You God alone. What I could offer would never measure up to what You have done for me on the cross. You are the lover of my soul. I surrender both the pain and the pleasure of my circumstances. I surrender the despair and utter pain of letting go of what could have been. I give you my grief and my loss.

In surrendering, all is given but all is gained. Release your burdens, release your fears, and release your treasured possessions. Give them to Jesus. In that moment of loss and barrenness only the comfort of His loving arms can satisfy you. In that moment, and 'moment' may be figurative, for it can last for years; nevertheless, in that moment surrender it all. When all is given, all is received.

Have you felt His mighty wind? Have you felt His glory descend? Have you felt His kiss? Have you felt Him caress your hair? Have you heard Him call your name?

The sweet joy of surrender is what you find, once your grief is truly laid down. A place of bliss and unfathomable glory is what He wants to reveal to you; unspeakable peace and love, liquid love being poured out all over you. His presence will overwhelm you. The price of surrendering may be high. It may cost you everything, and yet it is free. It becomes a sweet sacrifice of surrender.

Oh my Lord, only one life I have to give, and that life I freely give, for all I have is from You. All I have is Yours, You in me, and I in You: the hope of glory. Freely you have received, now freely give. Surrender it all. What is He asking of you?

Surrender it all; the pain lasts only for a moment; the pleasure, forevermore.

Reflection:

What has your faith cost you? How have you grown from the suffering you have walked through?

A Mother's Heart Cry

Psalm 62: 5-8
My soul, wait silently for God alone,
For my expectation is from Him.
He only is my rock and my salvation;
He is my defense;
I shall not be moved.
In God is my salvation and my glory;
The rock of my strength,
And my refuge, is in God.
Trust in Him at all times, you people;
Pour out your heart before Him;
God is a refuge for us.

Father, in the midst of my brokenness, in the midst of my utter despair, I throw myself on Your mercy. I lay prostrate and still before You. I surrender all again and again. Though you slay me, I will yet praise You. In my darkest hour, as my mother's heart breaks, I call out to You my Lord, my Maker. You alone can rescue; You alone can redeem. You alone can change the darkness to light. Though many people mean well, they don't understand and how could they. To understand is to know; it is to experience. Yet Father, I find myself in this place where daggers have attacked my heart; daggers that were targeted for me. Daggers that were meant to destroy, daggers that the enemy laced with venom. Yet in my lowest of lows, I raised up my voice even if just to a whisper and declared You, oh Lord are faithful. You, oh Lord will snatch me from the devastation of loss and pain, from the devastation of my loved ones' poor choices.

When the pain was so great and oppression surrounded me on every side, when I opened my mouth yet no sound would come out; in His gentle and loving way, He spoke: "Just breath." For breathing was all I could do. To concentrate on my next breath was all I could handle. As I continued to wait in His presence, strength would rise up again in me, His strength. He is my strength and my shield, my strong tower, the righteous run to Him and are safe.

You reached down from on high and took hold of me. You drew me out of deep waters. You rescued me from my powerful enemies, from my foes who were too strong for me. They confronted me in the day of my disaster, but You oh Lord were my support. You brought me into a spacious place; You rescued me because You delighted in me. Psalm 18: 16-19 In the midst of your devastation, welcome Him into your chambers. Let Him wrap His arms around you. His loving kindness is truly better than life. He wants to reveal His great love towards you. He wants you to know Him as your Daddy God, your Abba, your Husband, and your Lover. He wants you to be intimately acquainted with Him, the lover of your soul.

Although the pain of my loved ones' choices remains; He lifted the oppressive weight. When waters rage and the torrents assail me again, I crawl into my secret place, intimately acquainted with Him. He has changed my heart. For I thought I knew Him, but now I know there is so much more. His love is multi-faceted. In His presence I will stay.

Lord, I am the apple of Your eye, hidden in the shadow of Your wings. Forever my love is Yours. As for my children, they are Yours. Do what You need to do, but Lord, rescue them from the fires of hell. Rescue them from their own

stubborn, willful ways. Father, I declare Your Word over them; Lord direct their hearts into God's love and Christ's perseverance. 2 Thessalonians 3:5 You are my delight oh Lord, I will rest in the shadow of Your presence. May my life be a continual praise offered up to You, for I will not give the Lord that which cost me nothing. Abba, I love you. In Your presence I will stay.

Give us help from trouble, for the help of man is useless. Through God we will do valiantly, for it is He who shall tread down our enemies. Psalm 60: 11 & 12

Reflection:

Ask the Holy Spirit to pray through you and write down what He reveals. In this you will be praying the will of the Father. Respond to His words from your heart and make it a prayer to Him. In your times of desperation, He wants to reveal Himself to you. Don't allow the enemy to steal this time with the Lord. "Lord I ask You to pray through me."

Before I Was Afflicted

Psalm 119:67
Before I was afflicted I went astray,
But now I keep Your word.

Father of all hope and comfort, in Your mercy You have found me. Though I was lost in circumstances and despair, Your love reached down and saved me from pain that was too great for me. You rescued the one You love. You taught me to love Your law. In desperation, I looked up and found the One my heart loves; the One I was created to be with. Your Spirit and Your word has found me and rescued me. You lifted me out of the mire that was set as a trap for me.

In the midst of utter loss and destruction, You taught me to look upon the Spirit of God and to rely upon the Word of God. You have filled me with joy and hope anew. Joy I never knew existed. In love, You brought many sons to glory.

In pain, You resurrect life. The hearts of men You make like Your own. Your passion is our redemption. You stand in the gap and bring us to love; the love of the Father. It is a costly love; love that snatches us from despair, and molds us to the heart of the Father.

In desperation He found me. He has rescued me from pain too great. Pain meant to consume me. Yet the passionate love of my Father filled me. He has burned His passion upon my heart. In the midst of pain, He has become my burning passion.

Now I live to make Him known. He is worthy of it all. Before I was afflicted, I went astray. Before I was afflicted, I knew not of the passionate, fiery love of the Father.

Yes, it was good for me to be afflicted so that I could learn of His decrees. His faithfulness is my reward. I've been made whole in the arms of my Father.

In the midst of your pain, He wants to reveal His burning love for you. The sacrifice of sweet surrender is painful for a moment, but His burning heart of love will change you for eternity.

It is good for me that I have been afflicted, that I may learn Your statutes. Psalm 119:71

Reflection:

How has your heart learned to trust Him through your affliction?

Write out your heart's response to the journey that He has had you go through.

The Heart of the Father To His Beloved Bride

Let Me Embrace You

Psalm 34:18
The Lord is near to the brokenhearted and
saves those crushed in spirit.

My beloved daughter, rest in My arms. Let Me embrace you. Be still in My arms of love. The storms will pass. Let Me secure you in the storms of life. I am your Father, and you are My beloved daughter.

My heart breaks for you. My child, come to Me. Let Me love you through it all. I will rescue you. Daughter, though you pass through the fire you will not even smell like smoke. Let Me embrace you.

My beauty you have gazed upon. Continue to bask in My love. My healing is yours. I will heal you. Your spirit will soar. I will make you a teacher to the teachers because you have been taught by the Master teacher. Your lovely face is what I see. My beloved, draw Me into your chambers of love, into your presence.

"Fear not, for I have redeemed you; I have called you by your name; You are Mine. When you pass through the waters, I will be with you; and through the rivers, they shall not overflow you. When you walk through the fire, you shall not be burned, nor shall the flame scorch you. For I am the Lord your God, the Holy One of Israel, your Savior.
Isaiah 43:13

Week Four

AGONY

1. Prayer to Release Our Children From A Spirit of Judgment and Selfcenteredness

2. The Arms of My Maker

3. Numbness

4. Cry Out

5. Take Me I Am Yours

6. Needless Casualties of War

7. The Heart of The Father To His Beloved Bride

Prayer to Release Our Children From A Spirit of Judgment and Selfcenteredness

Father, in the Name of Jesus, I come before You and ask You to cleanse my children with Your blood. Wash over them and purify them of sin. Father, have mercy on them. Forgive them of self-centeredness and judgments towards others. I bind the spirit of judgment and self-centeredness working against them. I command those spirits to be removed from their lives. I render them null and void. Lord, reveal to them that having an attitude of judgment opens them to a judgmental spirit. By the power of the Holy Spirit, let them cling to You, Lord, and let go of all judgments they are holding on to.

Father, heal up their broken hearts and bind up their wounds. Psalm 147:3

Reveal to them the love of the Father. I ask that You would show Yourself strong on their behalf. Let them know You are working in their lives. Father, increase in them. Draw their hearts to You. In the authority of Jesus Christ, and by the power of the Holy Spirit, I release the power of the spoken Word of God over my children. I declare that the same power that raised Jesus from the dead is at work in them. Romans 8:11 I decree that Jesus has defeated and dethroned the power of the enemy at the cross. Colossians 2:15 I use my authority given by Jesus, and I bind your power, devil, over my children and grandchildren. Devil, leave them alone. They are washed in the blood of Jesus. I bind and break every stronghold the enemy has over them. I speak to the spirit of judgment and self-centeredness and command it to be removed from their lives. I speak to that mountain and tell it to go in

Jesus name. I release my loved ones to Jesus. I release a blessing over my loved ones. I decree and declare that they are strong in the Lord and in the power of His might. Ephesians 6:10

My loved ones seek Your face daily. They walk with the wise and grow wise. Pro. 13:20 They have been taught of the Lord, and great is their peace. Isaiah 54:13

They number their days and have gained a heart of wisdom. Psalm 90:12 They rejoice always, they pray without ceasing, and in everything they give thanks. 1 Thessalonians 5:16-18 My loved ones do not judge others, they extend mercy, and mercy they shall find. James 2:13 The praise of God is in their mouths and a double-edged sword is in their hands. Psalm 149:6

Father, I stand in agreement, that Your Word will not return unto us void, but it will accomplish what You desire and achieve the purposes for which You sent it. Isaiah 55:11 I stand in the authority of Your Word, which does not change. It stands eternal. Psalm 119:89 You carry out the words of Your servants and fulfill the predictions of Your messengers. Isaiah 44:26 I declare that the mountains in my family's lives have been removed! You said that if I believe and doubt not that I can have what I have spoken. Mark 11:24 Therefore I stand and declare that the promises of the Lord for my family stand true. I believe, therefore I shall receive. In the mighty name of Jesus I pray. Amen!

The Arms of My Maker

Matthew 11: 28-30
Come to Me, all you who labor and are heavy laden,
and I will give you rest. Take My yoke upon you and learn
from Me, for I am gentle and lowly in heart,
and you will find rest for your souls.
For My yoke is easy and My burden is light.

Father, though an army besieges me, and arrows pierce my heart, Your unending love flows like a river to the very core of my being. Because of Your great love I stand. Wounded? Yes, but not defeated. Though the enemy ruthlessly attacked and caused such anguish, such despair, such tragic loss, that words can barely describe it. Yet the Lord was my confidence. When I could go on no more He carried me on eagles wings. When I could see no more, He gave me vision to see. He truly was my strong tower. I ran to Him, and I was safe. Now as I sit and ponder the years gone by, I know I will sing again, I know His love like I've never known it before. But for now it's okay to rest. Rest my soul, rest. Sitting in His lap, resting in the arms of My Maker.

In my distress I called upon the Lord, and cried out to my God; He heard my voice from His temple, and my cry came before Him, even to His ears. Psalm 18:6

Reflection:

How has the Lord strengthened your heart in the midst of great trials? In what tangible way has He revealed Himself to you?

Numbness

Psalm 77: 1-4
I cried out to God with my voice To
God with my voice; and He gave ear to me.
In the day of my trouble I sought the Lord; my hand was
stretched out in the night without ceasing;
My soul refused to be comforted.
I remembered God, and was troubled; I complained,
and my spirit was overwhelmed. You hold my eyelids
open; I am so troubled that I cannot speak.

When you've willingly poured out your life, like a drink offering; when you've selflessly given all you have to give, and then given some more; when you've devoted all your time, all your energy, all your money, all of who you are in selfless love, all was required; all was given.

I sit here in brokenness of heart; devastation so deep, numbness is all that arises. From time to time torrents of tears come rushing out, and then as if an invisible hand goes up, it all comes to a halt. As suddenly as the tears began they abruptly stopped. As the tears stopped I sat in numbness, in stillness; staring out into the vast unknown. I sit alone, surrounded by the stillness of air around me. Intensity of pain so high, that the Lord will
only allow a little pain at a time to be released. Overwhelming pain. I've been taken from! Stolen from! Maliciously and purposefully destroyed! Shattered dreams lying all around me, dreams of what could have been, what almost was, but can never be anymore.

Curiosity and secret rebellion led to a web of deception, a trap designed to destroy. As principles and values began to wane those I loved drifted further off course. While corruption enticed, traps laced with venom destroyed them. Destroying everything that was built in them. Taking all there was to take. Stripping of all decency, keeping them dependent on their ill-gotten substances. Confused, confounded and controlled by a web of demonic deception with one assignment: to utterly destroy them, to utterly destroy me.

Only the all-powerful hand of Almighty God could rescue them from such a situation. He did. From a thankful, yet broken and devastated heart, I write, allowing my pen to put down, what my heart and lips cannot seem to speak.

Whom have I in heaven but You? And there is none upon earth that I desire besides You. My flesh and my heart fail; But God is the strength of my heart and my portion forever. Psalm 73:25 & 26

Greater love has no one than this, than to lay down one's life for his friends. John 15:13

Reflection:

Our trials, devastation, and losses can in no way be compared to what Jesus' ultimate sacrifice has done for us. Yet we find comfort in knowing He understands us and has compassion for us. In what way have you related to John 15:13? How have you laid down your life for others?

Cry Out

Psalm 18: 4 & 5
The pangs of death surrounded me,
And the floods of ungodliness made me afraid.
The sorrows of Sheol surrounded me;
The snares of death confronted me.

I stand before the face of the Lord with wrenching pain and states of numbness. How can I stand and smile, laugh and move about as if there's not a care in the world? Meanwhile deep within I am broken, aching with pain; dying to live, living to die. I was as a woman forsaken in brokenness and loss while wicked attacks from the enemy were launched at my soul.

Torrents of pain then waves of healing interchanged back and forth. The Lord's healing presence was gently healing me, as I walked through the valley of despair.

Waves of healing, like a gushing downpour surged over me, then eases back to a light gentle rain. Waves of healing cascaded in, as the crest toppled over, then receded back to stillness.

Mighty rushing waters, bring back what was stolen. I stand before You in worship, arms lifted, yet internal storms raging. Invisible to those around me, yet my heart speaks while my lips remain silent.

To my Lord all is exposed, all is bare before Him. In silent restoration, in outcries of mercy, the undoing is being redone. I know my Maker will restore the devastation.

In this I take confidence, though, for now it's this valley of the shadow of death I must walk through. Although the day of darkness, with its desire to overtake you is at hand; the day of our Lord will prevail with authority and power to restore you.

Cry out! All is not lost. With whatever breath remains within you cry out! He is coming; the scepter is in His hand. Cry out, you belong to the King, the King of glory.

Heaven hears, heaven responds, even if all you have left is the countenance of a solemn face. Look up with the eyes of your heart and cry out. Hear, O Lord, when I cry with my voice! Have mercy also upon me, and answer me. When You said, "Seek My face," My heart said to You, "Your face, Lord, I will seek." Psalm 27:7

Reflection:

Ask the Holy Spirit to direct you to a Psalm. Read and meditate on what He shows you. Now write from your spirit back to the Lord. He will direct you if you ask Him to. This is vital in the healing of your inner wounds.

Take Me I Am Yours

Habakkuk 3: 17 & 18
Though the fig tree may not blossom, Nor fruit be on the
vines; Though the labor of the olive may fail, And the
fields yield no food; Though the flock may be cut off from
the fold, And there be no herd in the stalls— Yet I will
rejoice in the Lord, I will joy in the God of my salvation.

Though you see a land of barrenness, and your arms feel the empty coldness of death; in obedience to Jesus, make a decision to rejoice in God your Maker. Rejoice in the God of your salvation. He is your strength, and will turn your barrenness to fruitfulness; and your death to life.

Be still and know that He is God. Ps. 46:10 He is waiting for you. You are His heart's desire; His cherished possession. The King of the universe longs to be with you. The Father is looking for you to stop your activity amidst all your pain and be still in His presence. Surrender all to Him. He wants to lavish His love upon you, and take you higher than you've ever been.

Father, burn Your love within me. Let the fire of Your eyes burn through me and brand me with Your intoxicating love. You said I am Your cherished possession. I yield myself to You. Take me, I am yours. Possess me. Let the wine of Your love fill and overflow me, that just my shadow on others would cause them to become drunk in Your love. Let me be a carrier of Your presence; Your heavy, weighty, presence. My heart cries out, "Seek His face," Your face, Lord I will seek. As I gaze upon Your beauty Lord, overtake me with Your presence. I surrender all to You.

Reflection:

Even though you look around and all you see is barrenness, look up with the eyes of your spirit. Ask the Lord to give you a revelation of how He views things. Now declare His view out loud, regardless of what you see in the natural. Write down what He has reveals to you.

Needless Casualties of War

Psalm 55:1, 3-5
Give ear to my prayer, O God, and do not hide Yourself
from my supplication.
Because of the voice of the enemy,
because of the oppression of the wicked,
for they bring down trouble upon me,
and in wrath they hate me.
My heart is severely pained within me,
and the terrors of death have fallen upon me.
Fearfulness and trembling have come upon me,
and horror has overwhelmed me.

No matter what, Lord, I still choose to praise You; NO MATTER WHAT. For You have my heart; You have my life. Though I am ridiculed, scorned and betrayed, You've never left me. You only grew stronger inside me. I feel the intense passion of Your love, while at the same moment the bitter betrayal of loved ones. Bittersweet has taken on a new meaning. The overwhelming beauty and glorious bliss of Your presence envelope my being, while catastrophic devastation and needless casualties of war afflict my soul. Yet, I choose to lift up my eyes, in the intensity of pain and I lift my voice, crying out for You alone; my Rescuer, my Lover, my Husband, my Delight.

Beloved warriors of the King, I speak to the broken, captured slaves. Be released! In obedience to the Father lies your release. In trusting Him, you will flourish. I speak to the captured prisoners, "Be released, from your prison." If the Son makes you free, you shall be free indeed. John 8:36 I declare that restoration will come to your house and the blinders will fall. I claim your eyes for Christ, to see Jesus and His beauty in the midst of your pain. I declare hearts will be united, tied to His heart. I declare minds to be bound to the mind of Christ. I declare a new generation.

Beloved, the Lord has called you His own. Do not despise this grave devastation that has hit your home. Though you may feel grieved in spirit, though your heart is severely pained within, and overwhelming horror is all around you, run and cling to the arms of your Maker. Let Him defend you and heal you. He will give voice to your loss and you will raise up His standard against the enemy of your soul. You will rise above the chaos; you will rise above the disaster and reclaim what is yours. You will be found faithful and the Lord will ransom and redeem your life from the pit.

Reflection:

Write out your heart's cry. Don't allow the catastrophe to dictate to you.

Take the time to write out your heart's cry to the Lord. Then ask Him what to do. Is it time to take a stand or is it time to rest in His presence? We must learn how to yield to the Holy Spirit for direction. There is a proper time to weep and a proper time to fight.

The Heart of The Father To His Beloved Bride

My beloved daughter, draw near to Me. I understand your pain. I know your heartache. Bring Me all your fears and broken dreams; dreams for your children, dreams for your family. The pain is too great and you were never meant to carry it alone. So come, and in your brokenness let Me restore hope and life back to you.

For you My beloved are My most cherished possession. My arms are open for you. Come and be with Me. Let Me heal and transform you. In My presence there are pleasures forevermore. Give Me your children, and trust Me. For I know the plans I have for you, plans for your future and hope. Cast all your cares before Me and I will rescue you from this pit that seems so unbearable.

CATHY COPPOLA

Week Five

RESTORATION

1. Prayer For Hearts To Extend Forgiveness

2. Forever His

3. God Is Faithful To His Promises

4. One Who Pleases God

5. Divine Love

6. Abba Father, How I Love You

7. Come Away My Bride

Prayer For Hearts To Extend Forgiveness

Father, You said, Call upon Me in the day of trouble, I will deliver you and you shall glorify me. Psalm 50:15

Father, I call upon You now. I stand in the gap for my children and ask for Your mercy towards them. You are my refuge and my strength, a very present help in trouble. Psalm 46:1 I lift up my children before Your throne. Have mercy on them according to Your loving kindness and tender mercies. Blot out their transgressions. Psalm 51:1 Cause them to desire truth in the inward parts, in the hidden parts make them to know wisdom. Psalm 51:6

Father, forgive them of their sin, they know not what they do. Luke 23:34 Teach them that when they sin, they sin against You. Psalm 51:4 Help them to be quick to repent from the heart. Open their eyes so they see their own faults and are not blind to their own ways.

Create in them a clean heart, O God and renew a steadfast spirit within them. Psalm 51:10 Cause them to desire truth and be obedient to Your word.

The sacrifices of God are a broken spirit and a broken and contrite heart, O God, You will not despise. Psalm 51:17 Create in them a heart after You Lord, a heart that is sensitive to Your Holy Spirit and that would not want to grieve You.

You said in Your word, who may ascend into the hill of the Lord? Who may stand in His holy place? He who has clean hands and a pure heart, who has not lifted up his soul to an idol. Psalm 24: 3 & 4 Cause my children to walk with a purity of heart and motive and when they are wrong let them quickly make it right.

Son of the living God, I trust in You. My hope and confidence remains unshaken, fixed and established in You. I have set my face like flint and I will not be moved. Isaiah 50:7

Thank You for hearing my heart's cry for my loved ones. I know Your word will not return unto me void, but will accomplish what You desire and prosper in the thing for which You sent it. Isaiah 55:11 I pray this in Your precious name Jesus. Amen.

Forever His

Romans 5:5
*Now hope does not disappoint, because the love of God
has been poured out in our hearts by the Holy Spirit
who was given to us.*

The place of intimacy with Jesus is a place of refuge from the storm. It is a place of sweet surrender where two hearts meet and love is the silent, yet understood, fragrance in the air.

To retreat to this place of intimacy is to find strength for the battle you may be in. When we find ourselves warring and storming the gates of hell, we must also find the place of sweet intimacy with the lover of our souls. Intimacy with the Father and warring in the spirit against evil are two necessities in our spiritual walk.

We must first learn to center our being with Jesus, who paid the price for us, and only then do we find true inner peace. In beholding Him we become like Him, for you become like what you behold. There is no sweeter joy, no sweeter place to be.

To be loved by the King and to love Him in return is His desire and this must become our desire as well. The Lord has brought me through many trials; yet, I consider everything a loss compared to the surpassing greatness of knowing Christ Jesus my Lord. Nothing can compare with knowing Him. His presence will overtake you and overwhelm you and you will find rest for your soul. Not just rest, but joy, even in the midst of your circumstances.

The price to pay for intimacy is high, yet it doesn't compare to His surpassing greatness, the greatness of really knowing Him. I am my Beloved's and my Beloved is mine. I have been captured and captivated; embraced and lovingly surrounded by His presence. Inwardly and outwardly He is all I taste and see and hear. He is my One and Only. I have been ruined for the ordinary. Oh how He loves me!

You may ask, "Why so happy?" Because I've tasted and I've seen that the Lord is good. I've been through the river, through the fire, and have come out through to the other side; the flame has not set me ablaze. This world has nothing for me, to live is to die, to die is to gain. In dying we gain Him.

There is a river of joy overflowing from the fountain of life within me. In my trials, I've met the King, I've met my Lover, my Husband, my Maker. In my trials, I've met the Author of love. Although I thought I knew Him, I did not know Him like I do now. Although I had eyes to see before, He opened my eyes to really see. My Lover has wooed me to His side. How can I now live the same? How can I now move and be and have my being? How can I ever be the same? He has taken me into His intimacy. He has captivated me with His love. I am forever His.

I am my beloved's and my beloved is mine.
Song of Songs 6:3

Reflection:

Are you enjoying intimacy with the Father? Ask Him to draw you into His inner chambers of love. Ask Him to open your eyes to really see Him with the eyes of your spirit. He has so much more to give you; so much more to reveal to you.

God Is Faithful To His Promises

Romans 4:3
Abraham believed God,
and it was accounted to him for righteousness.

What did Abraham believe God for? He had a promise from God. A promise that said he would be the father of many nations. Yet as it stood, Abraham had no child.

After he received a word from God, many, many years went by and his word from God still had not come to pass. During this time, Abraham had done some things in his own strength. He made some mistakes. He left the place where God told him to go because of a famine in the land. He said that his wife Sarah was his sister; he took Hagar as a second wife and had Ishmael with her. These are just a few of the things that Abraham did that were not directed of the Lord.

He was human like you and me. Although, he is credited as being the father of faith, we can see that he also made mistakes, but God in His mercy, came to his rescue. I believe this is because God knew that Abraham's heart was to serve the Lord. He really did want to be obedient. God was also growing his faith.

The Lord is not a respecter of persons. In what area is He growing your faith? What has God promised you? When God gives us a promise, we must contend for it. The enemy of your soul doesn't want the plan of God to be fulfilled in your life. He will work overtime because he wants you to get discouraged and frustrated. His hope is that you will eventually give up.

God's plan in your life is for you to bring Him glory. Each one of us has a specific destiny. When we follow God's plan, we will be operating to our fullest potential, which will bring satisfaction to our souls. The enemy knows this and he contends for it. If God has spoken something to your heart, you must stand for it and wait, even if it takes a long time. When God gives revelation of our future, we must be very careful to guard these promises and contend for them until they come to pass.

The enemy also heard of the plan of God for Abraham's life. God said to him, "Abraham, you will be the father of many nations. I will make your offspring like the dust of the earth." Gen. 15:5 The enemy heard this too, and tried to stop it. Because Abraham ultimately cooperated with God, his destiny was fulfilled. He received what was promised.

What about you? Have you believed what God has spoken to you? Have you been waiting for a promise to come to pass? Do not get weary in well doing. And let us not grow weary while doing good, for in due season we shall reap if we do not lose heart. Galatians 6:9

There will be many discouraging moments along the way. There will be times when you doubt if you have correctly heard God. Abraham felt the same way at times. Yet he never wavered in the promise.

What promise in your life are you hanging on to that seems dead? What has God impressed on your heart, yet circumstances seem to make it impossible for the promise to come to pass? We need to get our eyes off the circumstances and stand firm on what has been promised. God gives life to the dead and calls things that are not as though they were. Romans 4:17 Speak to what seems dead. Tell it to come to life! Remember the same spirit that raised Christ from the dead, lives and dwells in your mortal body. Romans 8:11 That SAME Spirit lives in you. You can't, but, Christ in you CAN!

Rise above your circumstances. Speak to the mountains; tell them to move. What has God has promised you? Declare it aloud. Contend for your promise. Remember in the book of Joshua ten people said no, it couldn't be done, and two said, yes, it can be done. The two saw the same giants that the other ten saw. They saw the same mountains. They weren't super humans. They had a choice. Would they activate their faith, or succumb to fear. We have the same choice.

We either choose to believe God's promises and contend for them even when it seems impossible; or we give in and give up and settle for less than what was promised to us. The choice is ours. God won't make you do either one. We have to choose. Against all hope Abraham in hope believed and so became the father of many nations, just as it had been said to him, "so shall your offspring be." Romans 4:18

Faith requires something of us. It requires us to believe even against all hope. Even when there is nothing on the outside, to be hopeful for, we must choose to put our hope in Christ. Circumstantially, there were no signs of hope in Abraham's case. Yet, against all hope he still believed in the GOD OF HOPE and he received his promise.

Without weakening in his faith, he faced the fact that his body was as good as dead, since he was about a hundred years old, and that Sarah's womb was also dead. Yet he did not waver through unbelief regarding the promise of God, but was strengthened in his faith and gave glory to God, being fully persuaded that God had power to do what he had promised. Romans 4:19-21

The Lord brought revelation to me one morning as I was reading this verse. I had read this verse many times before, but this time the Lord highlighted the very first part to me, *Without weakening in his faith, he faced the fact.* We can face the facts and still not waver in our faith!! The facts may say, you are not making enough money to do what God has told you to do. The facts may say that you can't change someone else's mind, therefore what you are hoping for is hopeless. The facts may say too much time has gone by, you are too old, it's too late, you are too far behind.

The facts are just that, facts. But the word of God says, let God be true and every man a liar. If God said it, it will be. Get behind what He said. We can face the facts, just don't get hung up on them. Facts are known to change. At one point people thought the world was flat. They thought it was a fact but facts change, truth remains the same. God's word is truth.

What has He spoken to you? Stand on it. Believe for it. Declare it out loud in prayer.

Share it with others who will agree with you and contend with you until it comes to pass. Believe for what He has promised you. Ask Him for your personal promise. Once you get it, don't let go of it. With faith and patience we will inherit God's promises.

Reflection:

Regardless of the condition of your circumstances, write out what God has spoken to you. Write the scripture promises next to it. Now meditate on this and do not all allow your heart to waver in unbelief. Speak your promise out loud into the atmosphere and believe that God will bring it to pass in His perfect time.

One Who Pleases God

Genesis 5:21
And Enoch walked with God; and he was not,
for God took him.

Hebrew 11:5
By faith Enoch was taken away, so that he did not see
death; he was not found, because God had taken him;
for before he was taken, he had this testimony;
that he pleased God.

Enoch walked with God. Before he was taken, he was commended as one who pleased God. How is your walk? Are you dialoging with the creator of your soul as you walk this life out? Could it be said of you that you are one who pleases God?

Since faith is what pleases God, do you have faith in knowing God loves you and that God is pleased with you? You are His creation; He fashioned you and made you into His own image. Remember, we are not loved by God because of our measure of success, but because He first loved us. Many believers are not sure of His love for them. They cannot get past their sense of being unworthy of His love and it becomes a blockage to the entrance of God's heart towards them.

None of us are worthy in ourselves. Only because of God's love towards mankind can we boast and this not in ourselves, but only in Him. Yet the enemy of our souls tries to keep believers in bondage, feeling unworthy of His love. This is a lie and a trap.

Can you honestly say, "God delights in me?" It is His desire that we delight in Him for He delights in us as His creation. Only when you know, deep within your spirit, that the creator dearly loves you, can you confidently say, "God delights in me." Only when we have had a revelation of His heart towards us, will we better understand the depths of His mighty love for us. When we have an understanding of His love for us, it causes our hearts to soar and embrace that love. We were created for this; created for love.

One who is an orphan knows of the estrangement they feel and the rejection of not belonging. Only by His divine revelation can you understand that you are His cherished possession, His esteemed treasure. A prince knows he is headed to be a king and acts accordingly. We too are kings and priests.

Unfortunately many believers do not understand their place in the Kingdom and do not act accordingly. We must receive the understanding of our kingdom reign by His word and by revelation, or we walk in this life feeling alone, estranged, and unwanted.

Ask Him for a deeper revelation of His heart towards you. He wants to reveal His unconditional love for you. When you know His love, you will walk in a manner that pleases Him, knowing that He is also pleased with you.

Abba Father, thank You for Your great love towards me. Thank You that Your love is not dependent upon my works or skills or success, but because of Your great love for mankind. Thank You that while I was yet a sinner You died for me. You saved me and called me Your own. Thank You that You have filled my life with a sweet

smelling fragrance that comes from knowing You are mine and I am Yours. You have revealed Your unending love towards me, and I am overwhelmed by Your indescribable love.

Enoch was commended as one who pleased God. I know You are pleased with me, not because I walk in perfection, but because I walk in faith. I am Yours and You are mine. The two cannot be separated. I am unified and made one with You. Lord, this revelation is only by Your supernatural power in my life. Thank You, Daddy. I ask for more revelation of Your heart, more revelation of Your love.

But without faith it is impossible to please Him, for he who comes to God must believe that He is, and that He is a rewarder of those who diligently seek Him. Hebrew 11:6

Reflection:

Our heart's desire is to please God. Ask Him what needs to change in your life. Be obedient to what He tells you to do. Now stand in faith against all odds and watch Him move.

Divine Love

Psalm 42: 1 & 2
As the deer pants for the water brooks,
so pants my soul for You, O God.
My soul thirsts for God, for the living God.

In my darkest hours, when catastrophe surrounded me, and my heart ached with pain, the love of the Father found me with waves of liquid love crashing in again and again. He has wooed me into His inner chambers. His intoxicating love filled me in my inner most being and now spills over. I cannot contain it. Such great pain has met such great love.

You, O God are the reason I stand. You are the reason I live. In the intensity of pain, I turned my eyes to my Lover and my heart became overwhelmed by the liquid love my Daddy God poured over me. For I know that My Lover is mine and I am His. Your love is better than wine; more enticing than the riches of this world. If I were to lose all, yet only have You, I would still have all. You have consumed my heart. My soul clings to my Lover.

I will not let You go. Because of this great adversity, You reached down from on high and wooed me into Your inner courts. Now I have tasted and have seen how real and tangible the love of God is. I will never be the same. I have been ruined for the ordinary. I am walking in extraordinary love of which my soul sings. I have found the treasure; His divine intoxicating love. Though my circumstances have not changed, my heart has been set on fire. I am in love with the King of Kings.

Reflection:

Though your circumstances may not have changed, how have you changed? Abandon yourself to Him. Completely surrender your heart, even if you have done so one thousand times before. Let go and trust Him. He will never let you down.

Abba Father, How I Love You

Psalm 61: 1-4
Hear my cry, O God; attend to my prayer.
From the end of the earth I will cry to
You. When my heart is overwhelmed;
Lead me to the rock that is higher than I.
For You have been a shelter for me,
a strong tower from the enemy. I will abide
in Your tabernacle forever,
I will trust in the shelter of Your wings.
Lord, Your love consumes me.
It melts me and transports me to Your glory.

Abba, take me away with You. You are my soul's delight. In Your presence there is abundant life. Where You lead I will follow. Oh how I love You. You are everything to me. You are my passion in pain and my longing in despair. My love for You Abba is increasing, like a burning fire; a flame all around me. Take me deeper into Your chambers. I am intoxicated by Your great love.

The waves of love and currents of passion are electrifying my very being. The great love of my Father consumes me. All to Jesus I surrender. All I need I've found in You. Take me away into Your chambers; Your chambers of love. As I sit in Your presence, the weight of Your glory falls all around me. Your weighty presence is healing me and lifting me to higher dimensions with You.

Then I hear You speak, "My daughter, welcome into My chambers. You are My beloved; My love, My bride. Let Me heal you and restore you. Let Me love you and make you whole. My love is all you need. It will satisfy your deepest longing. Just be still. Come into My chambers and be still."

You, O Lord, are faithful. I choose to stand upon Your faithfulness. I choose to believe that You, O God are my rescuer, my redeemer, my counselor, my friend. You will answer the deepest cry of my heart. Father, I bring my children to You. For You alone are faithful. Will You father them? Will You show them Your burning heart for them? Father, I trust You with them. Here they are Lord. As an act of my will I give them to You. Complete the work You've begun in them.

Reflection:

In the midst of your pain, tell Him that you lay all your concerns down at His feet and worship Him. Ask Him to take you deeper into His chambers of love. Write what He reveals to you.

The Heart of the Father To His Beloved Bride

Come Away My Bride

Lamentations 3:21-23
Yet this I call to mind and therefore I have hope: Because
of the Lord's great love we are not consumed, for His
compassions never fail. They are new every
morning; Great is Your faithfulness.

"Beloved, all is not lost. In agony of soul, cry out. All is not lost. The daggers that came against you, the deep anguish, the ripping and tearing of your soul were sent by the enemy to destroy you; yet you were found faithful. Though you were maliciously robbed, scornfully used, and intentionally crushed, you, My daughter, were like a wall that could not be destroyed. All is not lost, only rewarded.

The reward of the Lord is yours. Depths and riches that go beyond natural limits, I will give you. I will lavish you with the restoration of heaven; there is no earthly comparison. Your reward is great. You, my daughter, were faithful; all is not lost.

Come away my bride. Soak in my presence. For I am your beloved and you are Mine."

The Lord is near to those who are brokenhearted and
saves those who are crushed in spirit.
Psalm 34:18

Sometimes, though you give all of yourself and you do all you can to stop a tragedy from happening, devastation still occurs. Sometimes, the grief you experience is far too much for words. The love of a mother can never be outdone except by the love of the Heavenly Father. There is a time to war for your loved ones, but there is also a time to rest. Rest in the love of your Heavenly Father. Beloved, rest when you are instructed to, for the Lord sees your labor of love and His reward is with Him.

Week Six

PASSION

1. Prayer To Stand On Promises For Children

2. Enthralled By Your Beauty

3. The Pearl Of Great Price

4. Rest Between His Shoulders

5. Jesus Possess Me; I Am Yours

6. Sacrificial Worship

7. You Must Go Deeper Before You Go Higher

Prayer To Stand On Promises for Children

Father, I stand on Your word which changes not. You said, I will not violate my covenant or alter what my lips have spoken. Psalm 89:34 I believe therefore I will receive whatever I ask for in prayer. Matthew 21:22

Against all hope, Abraham in hope believed and so became the father of many nations, just as it had been said to him, "So shall your offspring be." Without weakening in his faith, he faced the fact that his body was as good as dead - since he was about a hundred years old - and that Sarah's womb was also dead. Yet he did not waver through unbelief regarding the promise of God, but was strengthened in his faith and gave glory to God, being fully persuaded that God had power to do what he had promised. Romans 4:18-21

Father, by Your Spirit I will not waver in unbelief concerning my loved ones. Even if things seem dead, I shall, against all hope, stand in hope and believe. Therefore I know and am fully persuaded that You have the power to do what You said You would do. I declare Your word: I will pour My Spirit on your descendants and My blessings on your offspring. Isaiah 44:3

Captives will be taken from warriors and plunder retrieved from the fierce. I will contend with those who contend with you and your children I will save. Isaiah 49: 24-25 I will put my laws on their hearts, and I will write them on their minds. Hebrews 10:36 The seed of the righteous shall be delivered. Proverbs 11:21 I stand on the word of God, which states: God gives life to the dead and calls those things which do not exist as though they did. Romans 4:17   I call my children and loved ones to life. I call them saved, redeemed, justified, sanctified, holy, and righteous children of God who walk not of their own will, but the will of the Father. Regardless of what circumstances dictate, I also glory in my sufferings, because I know that suffering produces perseverance; perseverance, character; and character, hope. And hope does not put me to shame, because God's love has been poured out into my heart through the Holy Spirit, who has been given to me. Romans 5:3-5

Who shall separate me from the love of Christ?   Shall trouble or hardship or persecution or famine or nakedness or danger or sword? No, in all these things I am more than a conqueror through Him who loved me. For I am convinced that neither death nor life, neither angels nor demons, neither the present nor the future, nor any powers, neither height nor depth, nor anything else in all creation, will be able to separate me from the love of God that is in Christ Jesus my Lord. Romans 8: 35-39

Therefore because of the love of God which has been poured out into my heart through the Holy Spirit, I will never be lacking in zeal, but will keep my spiritual fervor, serving the Lord. I will be joyful in hope, patient in affliction, faithful in prayer. Romans 12:11 & 12

I walk in confidence that what God said, He will also do. For God is not a man that He should lie, nor the son of man that He should change His mind. Does He speak and then not act? Does He promise and not fulfill? Numbers 23:19

The God of hope fills me with all joy and peace as I trust in Him, so that I may overflow with hope by the power of the Holy Spirit. Romans 15:13 I praise Your wonderful name. All glory, all honor, all praise belongs to You and You alone. Amen.

Enthralled By Your Beauty

Psalm 139:1
O Lord You have searched me
and You know me.

Man's greatest unspoken need is to be known and to be loved. Our heavenly Father already knows our desires, our drives and our needs. The all-loving Father loves you. The all-knowing, all-powerful, heavenly Father knows you.

When you awake He is there; when you work, He is there; when you rest, He is there. When you get anxious and insecure, He is there. He will never leave you nor forsake you. He understands your thoughts, and is acquainted with all your ways. His thoughts are always on you and His heart is burning for you.

My heart burns with passion and desire for you, for I have fashioned and formed you. I desire to be with you and to be desired by you. You are always on My mind. I thought about you before creation. I foreknew you and put My spirit on you. I love my created ones; you are the beloved of My beloved's. Do you hear Me beckoning you?

Come, sit, dwell with Me a while. Let Me love you, for you are My most treasured possession. I love you. I am love. Sit, wait and look upon Me; let Me gaze upon your lovely face. I am the sound that echoes through time. You can only know this sound by your spirit, for I the Lord, am Spirit. I am enthralled by your beauty; enthralled by your love.

Reflection:

The Author of your destiny is beckoning you to come sit with Him. How will you respond to His invitation to be still?

The Pearl of Great Price

Matthew 13: 45 & 46
Again, the kingdom of heaven is like a merchant seeking
beautiful pearls, who, when he had found one pearl of
great price, went and sold all that he had and bought it.

The Lord is my life, my strong tower, my Husband and my Maker. My soul leaps for joy at the mention of His name. I'm in love with the King. He has captured my heart. To be fully given to Him is my soul's desire. There is no storm He cannot still. There is no devastation or loss He hasn't already redeemed. I praise Him; the God who gives and takes away. For to live is death and to die is gain. Death has no hold on me.

I have tasted and I've seen that the Lord is good; so very good. May my life be a sweet sacrifice; a surrender unto God. My passion is but one, to become a continual dwelling in which God lives by His Spirit. I will surrender all, for the treasure I've found in Him, abandoning all else for the sake of following Him. My soul cries out "Abba Father". True riches, true joy, awaits the one who will embrace Him.

Yes, the Lord gives and takes away, and I count it all joy to praise Him in times of plenty and praise Him in times of lack; for the ravishing of my heart, where two hearts beat as one, no one can take away.

This place of soul surrender and heart security is the working of the Mighty King, the lover of my soul. All praise and glory and adoration be unto Him. I am His and He is mine. Blessed be the name of the Lord.

Don't let anything rob you from enjoying time with Jesus on a daily basis. Don't let anything or anyone steal your heart's focus on the greatest gift of all, God's only Son.

Reflection:

Jesus is our Pearl of Great Price. In what ways has He become close to your heart these past few months? What have you gone through that no one knows but Jesus? How has this brought you closer to Him? Write about it.

Rest Between His Shoulders

Deuteronomy 33:12
Let the beloved of the Lord rest secure in Him, for He
shields him all day
long, and the one the Lord loves rests between His
shoulders.

To know and to do are two different things. You may know the importance of being in His word daily, but unless you do it, it does you no good. His word instructs us to rest in Him and not only rest, but also to rest securely in Him.

This is much easier said than done when circumstances are difficult in your life. It takes a commitment of your will. It is easy to rest in Him, in His presence, when things are going well; but what about when they are not? How easy it is and how quick we are to become worried and stressed. This is not the will of the Father. We must learn to trust Him in all circumstances. He is waiting for us to take Him at His word. Let the beloved of the Lord rest. We must choose to rest in Him even when things are completely out of our control. Tell Him of your desire to obey and rest securely in Him. He will help you, but you must quiet yourself and choose to look to Him. Choose to not let your fears rule you, instead make a decision to rest securely in Him today.

Father, I make a decision of my will to not let circumstances rule me. I choose to rest securely between Your shoulders. I know You have the universe in Your hands. I choose to dwell in the faithfulness of God, and not allow the enemy of my soul to get me into a frenzy

with things that are out of my control. I am the beloved of the Lord.

Father, I quiet my heart. I still my thoughts and enter into the secret place of rest with You. I turn my attention and my focus on Your beauty, on Your love, and I rest in You. Your word says in Psalm 91:1 he who dwells in the shelter of the Most High will rest in the shadow of the Almighty. Your all encompassing beauty fills my mind, my emotions and my will. Because the Lord loves me, I rest securely between His shoulders. He embraces me with His loving arms.

Reflection:

Ask the Lord to encounter you with His presence. Put on worship music and sit or lie before Him and let Him encounter you. Then write what He reveals to you.

Jesus Possess Me; I am Yours

2 Corinthians 1:20
For all the promises of God in Him are Yes and Amen
to the glory of God through us.

Father, in the name of Jesus, I come before Your throne in humility to ask You to make me more like You. My desire is to be Christlike. I desire to be transformed from the inner man and to be transformed into Your glorious image. I am fully surrendered and yielded to Your Holy Spirit; to mold, prune, teach, discipline and transform me. I want to release the fragrance of Christ everywhere I go.

You said all the promises of God in Him are Yes and Amen to the glory of God through us. The promises You have made are found in You. They are manifested in my life as my life is hidden in You. For when I am in You, You will be glorified through me. Father, teach me how to remain in You. I understand that it is through the trials of life that I will be pruned and changed into a Christlike image, as long as I allow the inner work of transformation to be done. I recognize that when I ask to be made more like Jesus, I am inviting pruning, as well as opportunities, for me to say no to my flesh. Holy Spirit, I can't do this without You. I am calling on You ahead of time.

Quicken my spirit when the temptation comes. That instead of rebelling or running from the challenge, I would recognize it and partner with You so that Christ would work in me and transformation would happen. The external promises that are yes and amen will be in effect once the internal death to self is accomplished.

Lord, teach me Your ways. Teach me to be sensitive to following after You and not my flesh. Be glorified in and through me.

Israel suffered in Egypt and taskmasters were set over them to afflict them with burdens. But the more they afflicted them, the more they multiplied and grew. Exodus 1: 11 & 12

Spirit of God, my desire is to be more like You. Spirit of God, do what only You can do. Quicken me for the tests that lay ahead of me. When I'm afflicted and burdened, cause me to stay in the fragrance of Christ and grow. Cause me to multiply and grow in godly character and godly transformation. For then and only then will the promises of God truly be magnified in my life. The promises of God in Him are yes and amen to the glory of God in us.

Consider it pure joy, my brothers whenever you face trials of many kinds, because you know that the testing of your faith develops perseverance. Perseverance must finish its work so that you may be mature and complete, not lacking anything. James 1: 2-4

Reflection:

Are you counting it all joy? Let Him work in you so you will be complete, not lacking anything. In all things give Him praise and watch Him turn your sorrow into joy.

Sacrificial Worship

Luke 23:34
Then Jesus said, "Father, forgive them,
for they do not know what they do."
And they divided His garments and cast lots.

Beloved, look beyond your loved ones' sin and look to Me. Keep the eyes of your heart on Me. For I will lift the burdens you carry. You must look beyond the sin and carry them to My throne. You will be the one to carry your loved ones in the spirit. I will reconstruct the brokenness in their hearts. Your faith in Me is what pleases Me.

I use your faith and obedience to bring your loved ones to My throne and cause miracles in their lives. In faith, in joy and in confidence, bring them to Me and lay them at the altar, then just focus on My heart. Become lost in My love, for My love will free the captives and revive the dead. Your obedience to enter into worship is the key to your loved ones victory. For when they surrender and come back to Me, the work in the spirit will have been done and you will receive the rewards of a faithful worshiping warrior. For that is who you are, that is what I've called you to be.

So dance with Me, lover of My soul, dance with Me as I dance with you. Sacrificial worship; though it costs you, the rewards are countless. For in so doing you relate to Me, and My sacrifice for you, it cannot be weighed. Love them with the love of the Father, for I alone will rescue them; they are Mine.

Sometimes you must allow the foolishness that is bound in the hearts of loved ones and keep them in prayer on the altar of sacrifice. The Lord requires you to look beyond their sin and keep your eyes on Him. Forgive them, for they know not what they are doing. The deceiver may have blinded their minds for now, but the love of God is a mighty rushing wind and will restore their vision and their hearts. As for you, carry them in prayer and leave them at the altar. Worship Him in your loss and heaviness. He will free the enslaved prisoners you bring to Him. Have faith in Him. Believe Him. Lose yourself in His love and He will direct you. You will not be forsaken.

Reflection:

Ask the Holy Spirit to reveal to you whom you need to forgive. What pain or heartache has caused you to put a block between you and your loved one?

The Holy Spirit will search your heart if you ask Him to. Now forgive from the heart all those He reveals to you. Holding on to unforgiveness is too costly for you. Offer it as a sacrifice of praise unto Him, even if it is very difficult to forgive.

The Heart of The Father To His Beloved Bride

You Must Go Deeper Before You Go Higher

Proverbs 8:17
I love those who love Me, and those
who seek Me diligently find Me.

My heart is beating for you. I see you, I know you. Do not move from the shelter of My embrace. For My work is not yet finished. Deeper, deeper we must go. Don't be afraid of what will come next. I will be leading you. Continue your stillness before Me, for I am healing your inner man. I will move gently. You will feel stripped, defeated, utterly broken. For the layers of pain must be released. But you will not be alone. I know you intimately.

Together we will journey down this road to complete freedom. My love for you burns passionately. The flame will never go out. You have the fire of My Spirit within you, but you also have the gentleness of a dove. I see what you've been through. I will not forget. We must first go deeper before we can go higher. Because when you go higher, I want you to remain there and not falter. The higher I take you, the more you will be opposed, but the revelation of My love is greater.

We must go deeper before we go higher and heal the painful memories. We must heal the wounds that have only been bandaged, uncovering the disappointments so we can bring wholeness to them and set you free. You are a carrier of My Spirit. Where you go, I go. Never will I leave you. You will dance, you will sing, you will write of My love and you will teach. You will lead others to where you've been. You will touch many. The fire will be a blazing inferno and I will put it there; the fire of My love. Be still before Me and write, not works done in the power of flesh, but works of power taught in stillness.

Week Seven

DELIGHT

1. Prayer To Walk In The Fullness Of God

2. Worthy Of Him

3. Sons And Daughters

4. Rivers Of Living Water

5. Awaken Me To Hear

6. Love Incomprehensible

7. The Heart Of The Father To His Beloved Bride

Prayer to Walk in The Fullness of God

In the name of Jesus, I come into agreement with the power of the Holy Spirit. I declare out loud the living, active Word of God. You said that You would not violate Your Word, nor alter what your lips have spoken. Psalm 89:34 You said You are watching over Your Word to perform it. Jeremiah 1:12 Lord, perform Your Word now.

Father, I stand and intercede on behalf of my family. I bind up the strong man and prohibit him from interfering with this prayer. Matthew 18:18 I lift up my husband, children and grandchildren, those born and those not yet born. I lift them up to Your throne of grace. I declare that the King of Righteousness has come with healing in His wings: healing of emotions; healing of painful memories and healing of the body. Malachi 4:2

I declare that my loved ones have received Your healing and applied it to their area of need. I declare in faith that my family walks in the fullness of God daily. Father, let Your Kingdom come, let Your will be done on earth as it is in heaven. Matthew 6:9-13

I declare that my children are victorious. They are covered with the blood of Jesus. My enemies will cower before me and I will trample down their high places. Deuteronomy 33:29 I take the Word of the Lord and tear down every high thing that exalts itself above the name of Jesus and everything that would keep my children away from the Lord. 2 Corinthians 10:5

I bind up the strongman in their lives and command he stop harassing and enticing my loved ones in Jesus' name.

I submit to God, resist the devil and he must flee from me. James 4:7 Devil, flee from my family in Jesus' name. I declare that my children are on fire with the Lord and they passionately serve God. They seek Him with all their heart. My children are sensitive to the things of the Holy Spirit, and they no longer walk in compromise and complacency. They are victorious in Christ. They have the boldness of God in their mouths. I stand in agreement that all my children will be taught by the Lord and great will be their peace. Isaiah 54:13

Whoever attacks them will surrender to them. Isaiah 54:15 I apply the blood of Jesus over them. Father, surround them with godly influences. Capture their minds and fill them with the understanding of Your great love. I declare that they are new creatures in Christ, the old has gone, the new has come. 2 Corinthians 5:17 They have died to sin and have been raised in Christ and are now seated in heavenly places. Ephesians 2:6 The same Spirit that raised Christ from the dead lives in them, giving life to their mortal bodies. Romans 8:11

My children walk in humility with great favor on their lives. Father, I bless my future generations. My family and future generations will walk in obedience to You and serve You all the days of their lives. I declare it and establish it by the spoken word, for You said, I shall declare a thing and it shall be established. Job 22:28 I pray all these things in Jesus' name. Amen.

Worthy of Him

Philippians 1:27
Whatever happens, conduct yourselves in a manner
worth of the gospel of Christ.

There comes a point in time in everyone's life when they must choose if they are willing to stand for truth and risk being alone, or going with the flow and being with the majority. In life it is not what happens to you that determines your destiny, it is what you do with what happens to you. When you realize that it is not circumstances that make you who you are, but it is your reaction to them that determines your destiny, that is when you start owning your future. When you determine that regardless of what comes your way, you will choose to respond in a way that pleases the Lord, in thought, word and deed. You begin to see that your future is a product of your daily decisions. As we all face trials, hardships and persecutions of every kind, it is critical not to let them determine your destiny. If you are not careful to resolve in your mind and heart that you will live a life surrendered unto the King and conduct yourself in a manner worthy of the gospel, you will be robbed of the Lord's destiny for your life. Remember, it is what you do with the adversities of life that determine your future. Your reaction to life's circumstances will determine whether you succeed or fail in fulfilling God's plan for you.

Father, regardless of what comes against me, regardless of who opposes me, be it one close or far, I have firmly resolved that I will live wholeheartedly for You, and I won't shrink back. My life is an expression of love back to You.

When it seems all have abandoned me and I am found in silence and all alone, You are the air I breathe, the song I sing and the passion beating within me. Lord, no matter what, I will serve You; even in the face of adversity, even if I have to walk this road of life alone. I have set my heart on You, Jesus. Your face is the face I see in every person. Your words are the words I hear in every conversation. I am Your bondservant, Your handmaiden. No matter what happens in this life, whether I am surrounded by many or by few, I will walk in a manner worthy of the gospel, for Christ is my King.

Father, I choose to release offenses that have crept into my heart. I ask You for forgiveness for my sinful reaction to another's actions. You are the One who looks at the heart, and I want to be found faithful. So Lord, I pray for those who persecute me and I bless those who curse me. I will respond to them knowing that You are watching my response. I desire to please You in my inner being. Lord, I release offenses and I walk in wholehearted devotion unto You, King of Kings and Lord of Lords.

Reflection:

No matter what may come against you today, make a commitment to the Lord that your response will be in line with the heart of the Father. When you learn to see others through His perspective, offenses can't take root. Tell Him in your own words and write it in your journal as a reminder to you.

Sons and Daughters

Galatians 4:6 & 7
And because you are sons, God has sent forth the
Spirit of His Son into your hearts, crying out,
Abba, Father!"
Therefore you are no longer a slave but a son,
and if a son, then an heir of God through Christ.

Father, thank You for sending the Spirit of Jesus into my heart. You are my Abba Father. I am no longer a slave. I once was a slave to self and sin. I once did not know who I was or where I was going. You came and redeemed me. You redeemed my life from the pit and prison of my own doing. I once thought I was selfsufficient and didn't need anyone. But You rescued me. You were patient and kind. When I cried out to You, You were right there. You picked up all my brokenness and began the years of mending me back together. Lord, thank You for never giving up on me, even when I gave up on myself.

Thank You for teaching me what "Abba Father" means. You became my Daddy and begun nurturing and speaking life to a bruised and broken reed. My heart is full of thanksgiving. I will never forget Your kindness and unending love towards me. I am no longer a slave but a daughter. I know that my Daddy longs to be with me. Your heart yearns for me. From everlasting to everlasting is Your love for me. I am your daughter and forever grateful I will be. I am lovesick for You, Lover of my soul. You have brought me into the family of God and have given me an inheritance. Though once I was estranged from You, now I am an heir of Christ. Abandoned to love. Lavished by Your love. May my life be a fragrant offering

poured back unto You, burning with the love You have poured into me. I lavish my love back to You and to those You bring to me. Lord, use me to bring others close to Your heart.

You shall love the Lord your God with all your heart, with all your soul, with all your mind, and with all your strength. This is the first commandment. And the second, like it, is this; You shall love your neighbor as yourself. There is no other commandment greater than these. Mark 12: 30 & 31

Reflection:

How is the greatest commandment evident in your life? Does your life exemplify being a slave or an heir? Ask Daddy God to draw you into His chambers of love and speak life over you. Sit in His presence and let Him reveal His heart towards you. Write what He shows.

Rivers of Living Water

John 7:37 & 38
If anyone thirsts, let him come to Me and drink.
He who believes in Me, as the scriptures has said,
out of his heart will flow rivers of living water.

Are you satisfied with your life, or do you believe there is more? There is a satisfaction only the Lord God Himself can bring. Only He can create thirst in you for Him and only He can satisfy that thirst. The waters He speaks of are waters of life; deep wells of passion and compassion for God and His creation.

Ask Him to let the rivers of living water flow from His heart directly to your heart and then flow out to those around you. The more you draw near to Him, the more He increases the flow of living water. The flow of life coming forth from your heart will be so full of joy and passion it should be difficult to contain it. This uncontainable love bubbles up within you and spills over to those around you. At times, the rivers of living water flowing from your heart feel like an explosion within you.

Lord, show me how to channel all this passion and the presence of Your indwelling Spirit so I can be used to bless those around me. Oh Lord, so many don't know You like this. So many people are walking around proclaiming Your name, but they are lifeless. Lord, use me to touch those around me with Your rivers of living water.

Maybe you're not experiencing this flow of living water. This is a good time to stop what you are doing and ask Him to create this in you. If you desire Him to cause your heart to bubble up with His joy, pray this prayer with me:

Lord, the truth be known, I am not experiencing that flow of living water from Your heart to mine. Lord, would You create in me such a hunger for You and satisfy my soul with rivers of water from Your heart? Thank You Daddy. I will wait in Your presence and watch You move in my life.

Reflection:

Are you drinking from the well of life and receiving life from Him? The condition of your heart will determine how often and how deeply you are drinking from His well. Ask Him to create in you a thirst for Him if you feel it is waning.

Awaken Me to Hear

Isaiah 50:4
The Lord has given me the tongue of the learned, that I
should know how to speak a word in season to him who
is weary. He awakens me morning by morning.
He awakens my ear to hear as the learned.

It is the Lord who awakens me morning by morning. He has stirred my inner man to hunger and seek after Him. There are many who are physically awake, yet spiritually asleep. If your desire is to be alive in Christ, to truly be awakened by Him in your spirit man, ask Him to draw you unto His heart. He is not a respecter of persons. His desire is to awaken you to hear from His heart.

A true communion and a true exchange is what transpires when you make fellowship with Him your priority. He will awaken your heart to hear His heartbeat. He longs for you to take every circumstance in life and have it become an instant dialogue between you and your Maker, therefore bringing you closer to Him. In doing so He fine-tunes you to hear from His heart, so you will respond to Him.

Father, Your word declares that You have given me the tongue of the learned, that I should know how to speak a word in season to him who is weary. Awaken me morning by morning; awaken my ear to hear as the learned. Lord, speak to me and cause me to hear You. Let me feel the Breath of Life, and awaken my spirit man to respond to the Holy Spirit. Today, no matter what I encounter, make me sensitive to bring all things to You in prayer, so I will hear

Your heart on each and every matter. Make me in tune to You Holy Spirit, and teach me so that I will know how to speak a word in season to him who is weary.

Reflection:

Ask Him to awaken you to His love. Ask Him to make you sensitive in the spirit so you will hear with your spirit, and know what to say in response.

Love Incomprehensible

John 15:9
As the Father loved Me, I also have loved you;
abide in My love.

Jesus, the Good Shepherd, calls me by name. I know His voice and the voice of another I will not follow. As the Father is in Jesus and Jesus is in the Father, I too am in Jesus. Therefore, the Father lives in me, and the Father and I are one. The scriptures cannot be broken; He leads me into all truth.

"Ask," He says, and "I will give you the Kingdom." His divine glory belongs to us. We are one with Him; God in us, the hope of glory. Bask in His divine love for you. You will understand His love as you yield yourself to Him and Him alone. Be still and know that He is God. As the Father has loved me, so have I loved you. With the same unending, self-sacrificing, incomprehensible love of God that was lavished on Jesus, so in turn, Jesus, with that same love, loves us.

We are loved as sons! We are loved with a love that comes directly from the heart of the Father. Even if you have experienced the depths of His great love, there is always more. It is multifaceted. It is the gift that keeps giving; always something new, never to be outdone. This is the Love the Father lavishes on us; the same love He lavished on His Son, Jesus Christ. Think about that.

The Father loves us with the same love and intensity that He loves His Son Jesus. Ask Him for a revelation of this great love. For the love of God will compel you to just "be" in His presence, knowing you are a son of God and the bride of Christ, His beloved.

The glory which You gave Me I have given them. That they may be one just as We are one. John 17:22

Reflection:

How has your life changed and become centered on Christ? Have you thanked Him for His great love towards you? How are you different this year compared to last year? Write down your heart's expression for what Jesus has done in you.

The Heart of The Father to His Beloved Bride

Songs of Songs 2:14
Let me see your face, let me hear your voice;
for your voice is sweet, and your face is lovely.

You are My beloved bride and I long to be with you. My heart desires your presence, My dove, My cherished possession. Come away with Me, My beloved, to the secret places of our dwellings. Let Me see your face, let Me hear your voice, for your voice is sweet and your face is lovely.

As much as we may desire the presence of God in our lives, it is overwhelming to think how the Creator of the universe longs to be with us, His created ones. You may desire to see His face and hear His voice, but remember, how much more He longs to see your face and hear your voice.

Come away with Him to the secret places and let Him ravish your heart with His love as you love Him in return. This is love; this is true intimacy. Hear Him beckon your heart to respond. Don't allow one more day to be stolen from you without experiencing His love being poured into your heart by the Holy Spirit.

Week Eight

GLORY

1. Prayer To Fight For Your Children

2. House Of Glory

3. Who Can Fathom His Love

4. That I May Know Him

5. The Alabaster Jar

6. Carried Along By My Father

7. The Heart Of The Father To His Beloved Bride

Prayer to Fight For Your Children

Exodus 14:14
The Lord will fight for you,
and you shall hold your peace.

Father, I bless Your name. I lift up my voice and declare, 'Hear, O Israel The Lord my God, the Lord is one.' Deuteronomy 6:4 There is no one holy like the Lord; there is no one besides You; there is no Rock like our God. 1 Samuel 2:2 All the earth shall worship You And sing praises to You; they shall sing praises to Your name. Psalm 66:4

My hope is built on nothing other than Christ, the solid rock, on which I stand. Your Word says that God is not a man, that He should lie, nor a son of man, that He should change His mind. Does He speak and then not act? Does He promise and not fulfill? Numbers 28:19 Therefore I am fully persuaded that what God has promised, He will also do. Romans 4:21

Joseph had to wait until his dream became a reality. I too am being tested to see the depth and the intensity of my love and faith in You Lord. Your word says, "Until the time that his word came to pass, the word of the Lord tested him." Psalm 105:19

Father, may I be found faithful. I am standing on Your promises for my loved ones. I will never give up. My hope and confidence is in You. Father, I take You at Your Word. I know that You are faithful and true. You do not change like shifting shadows. Forever Your Word is settled in heaven. Psalm 119: 89

I stand on Your Word which declares: My Spirit, who is on you, and My words that I have put in your mouth will not depart from your mouth, or from the mouths of your children, or from the mouths of your children's children from this time on and forever, says the Lord. Isaiah 59:20 &21

Father, I lift up my children and grandchildren to you. Deliver them from wicked and evil men. Strengthen and protect them from the evil one. Direct their hearts into God's love and Christ's perseverance. 2 Thessalonians 3: 2,3 & 5

Remove from their midst those who will entice them to evil actions and evil desires. Give my children a heart that desires Your will. Work in them to both will and do of Your good purpose. Philippians 2:3 Father, Your Word says, therefore, since we are receiving a kingdom that cannot be shaken, let us be thankful, and so worship God acceptably with reverence and awe, for our God is a consuming fire. Hebrews 12:28 & 29

Go before my family and me as a consuming fire, for I serve a King whose kingdom cannot be shaken! You will destroy my enemies and bring them down before me and I shall drive them out and destroy them quickly. Deuteronomy 9:3

I worship You and praise Your holy Name. In the name of Jesus I bind and break every evil spirit coming against my family. SATAN YOU'RE DISMISSED! I come against you in the name of the Lord. Amen.

House of Glory

Psalms 26:8
Lord, I have loved the habitation of Your house,
and the place where Your glory dwells.

Father, bring Your glory and dwell in my midst. Let Your glory fall. I want to be a temple that continually radiates Your glory; a vessel that hosts a deep well of Your presence. It's the glory that causes man's spirit to cease all action, and stills man's futility. Your glory that invades an atmosphere and overtakes all that are present with the thick weighty presence of the Lord. Let Your glory fall in my home Lord, so that all who enter will be absorbed in Your unseen, yet very noticeable presence. Your presence in me touches everyone I encounter, giving them a taste of the Almighty.

The presence of God dwells in my home and in my body. I am a walking spirit that radiates God's glory everywhere I go. This is His desire for all of us. Spending time with Him will bring this to pass. Don't let the busyness of life steal the riches from heaven the Lord longs to give you. In Him you have the fullness of life, riches forever more.

When Moses came down from Mount Sinai with the two tablets of the Testimony in his hands, he was not aware that his face was radiant because he had spoken with the Lord. Exodus 34:29

Reflection:

How much time in His presence and in His word are you spending daily?

The more time spent with Him the more radiant you will be for Him. Ask Him to reveal His glory to you. Make time for resting in His presence. Busyness will rob you of His glory.

Who Can Fathom His Love

1 Kings 18:24
The God who answers by fire, He is God.

Oh how He loves us. His love who can fathom? Who can comprehend? Who can measure it? Who can contain it? His love is a burning, consuming fire; burning away the dross and the pain of life.

Oh my God, you are love; burning, fiery, passionate love. Consume me; I am Yours. My heart beats with passion for You Lord. You have created in me deep, wells; wells of passion and compassion. Oh my God, I yearn for You. I need more of You Lord. Oh my God, my God, my God, You are all I need. You are all I want. Let me burn with a holy passion for You Lord. Who can contain the fiery passionate love of God? Who can measure it? Such love, such passionate love is too wonderful for words.

God set the burning bush on fire yet never consumed it. He burned that image into Moses' mind, yet did not cause him to burn. He causes the sin in our lives to burn up, yet He does not destroy us in the process. He burns His image into our spirits, and does not destroy us with shame or pain. His refining fire burns up the chaff and leaves us with purified gold. He then sets our hearts ablaze to burn for Him; the All-Consuming fire. He answers our heart's cry for He is the God who answers by fire.

His Living Word is like fire; like a hammer that breaks the rock. Is not My word like a fire, says the Lord, And like a hammer that breaks the rock in pieces? Jeremiah 23:29

Lord, Your word is like a fire and like a hammer that breaks the rock in pieces. Increase a spirit of burning within me that I would burn with passion in my heart for You, Living God. Consume all of me and make me like Your Son.

Reflection:

How do I develop a fiery love for God?

You must get to know Him first. Your love for Him will grow as you meditate on what He has already done for you. Sit before Him and ask Him to reveal His great love towards you. Dwell in His word and thank Him for His faithfulness. Ask Him to release in you a spirit of burning, baptizing you with His fire. Your heart will respond to Him.

That I May Know Him

Philippians 3:10
That I may know Him in the power of His resurrection
and the fellowship of His sufferings,
being conformed to His death.

Like Paul, we can't know Christ in resurrection power until we know Him in His suffering and death. Relationships deepen when you experience something on a personal level with someone. This creates an intimacy in your relationship. Intimacy creates more shared experiences and emotions which knit your hearts together, strengthens your bond and brings a security and loyalty deeper and more valuable to you than other friendships. This relationship becomes a safe place. A place you run to and find peace, acceptance, comfort, hope, renewed vision and joy.

As you run to the heavenly Father in times of trouble, you find His loving arms there to embrace you, comfort you and give you new hope. Intimacy with the Father grows as you take the initiative to run to Him. Although the Lord is always there, He is waiting for you to turn to Him and call on His name.

Abba Daddy is waiting for you to enter into intimacy with Him even in your difficult circumstances. His great love and patience for you is unending. He is beckoning you to call on His name. The more you experience Him in the secret places, the more He reveals to you His great love. During a time of difficulty, I chose to just be in His presence. I went to the Lord in worship and was telling

Him how much I loved Him. I just kept telling him over and over, "I love you, I love you, I love you."

His presence grew so sweet. He loves it when in our deepest time of need, we turn our eyes away from the problem and onto Him. His heart leaps for joy when, in the midst of pain, we can enter into His love. We were created for this, to enter into His chambers of love no matter what the external factors may be. As I continued to express my love for my Lord, I could feel His heart of love for me. I entered into the "sweet spot." Where, in the spirit, you have passed praying from your soul, your intellect, and begin praying spirit to spirit.

I began hearing Him say back to me, "I love you, I love you", with that, I told him, "I love You more." Even though I said those words, I knew that there was no possible way for me to love Him more! Yet it became this little sweet game between the Lord and me. I kept telling Him, " I love you more" and then gently laugh. I felt like He loved the whole thing. He didn't stop me and say, "That is doctrinally incorrect. I sent my Son to die for you, therefore you could never love Me more." He didn't state the obvious. He just let me play this little game with Him and I could feel His delight.

Whether you are facing a long intense battle or minor bumps in life, learn to get into the presence of the Lord. Let Him encounter you in a fresh way. Remember our battles in life are meant to produce intimacy with the Father if we'll let them. The key: enter into His rest and into His chambers of love. Regardless of external circumstances you will find Him. If you fellowship with Him in your suffering you will rise up with Him in resurrection power.

Sweet, sweet Jesus, how I love You. You are the air that I breathe, the calm in the storm, the warmth when I am afraid; You are my Lord. Everyday when I awake You are the first one to greet me and the last one there before I sleep. You lovingly whisper my name and call me Your own. When assaults and persecutions come, Your presence blankets my soul like a blanket warmed by the fire. Oh sweet Jesus, You are all I want. At the very sound of Your name, my heart leaps for joy, for You are my strong tower, my very sure salvation.

Let Your presence increase in my life. I want to burn for You. Passion for Jesus is the longing of my heart. Today and everyday, increase Your burning passion in me. Light a fire within and let it burn like never before. May Your flames of love consume me, and let me be Your love offering poured out to those around me. Jesus, take all of me. Eternally I stand, forever Yours. For You are my one desire and I am Yours.

Reflection:

Write your hearts response to this prayer above. Tell Him in your own words how much you love Him. Our sufferings may seem like death, but we will rise up in power if we do not let go of Him.

The Alabaster Jar

Mark 14:3
While Jesus was in Bethany,
at the house of Simon the leper,
as He sat at the table, a woman came having an
alabaster flask of very costly oil of spikenard.
Then she broke the flask and poured it on His head.

There is costly oil born of life's adversities for every believer; an alabaster jar filled with your fragrant offerings. The jar is not meant for you to keep, but for you to break open and lavish on Jesus. It is costly because it has cost you something; pain, loss and suffering. Yet to lavish your oil as an offering unto Jesus, is to break open the jar of your heart filled with pain, loss and suffering and give it all away. It is your extravagant form of worship.

Break open the flask of oil kept for Him. Pour out your heart unto Jesus. The pain and anguish will turn to expressions of love and exhilaration. He will fill you anew with unspeakable joy.

Once the flask is broken and poured out upon Him, your heart of love for Him will soar. You will be ruined for the ordinary, never to be the same again. Once you have given Him your all, He lavishes on you the riches of heaven.

His passion becomes your passion, for He is a God of passion. Your heart will beat to a different drum; to the beat of His heart. Don't waste your pain; give it all to Him, in abandoned, reckless love and passion. Break open your alabaster jar and lavish it on Him. It is your sacrificial offering; an exchange of passion for Him.

Father, because of Your loving kindness, I live. Because Your love is better than life, I live. I was in chains and You set me free. I was in prison and You released me. I was tangled in a web; Your tears washed over me, and brought me healing. You drew me to Yourself when everyone else abandoned me. You held me and never let me go. Now I rest between your shoulders. I've been kissed by the Son; Oh breath of heaven, hover over me. I am wrapped in Your beauty. I am embraced in Your loving arms; canopied by Your wings. Free to be Your created one. Captured by grace, surrounded by love, because of You, I live.

Reflection:

Don't let fear, shame or loss, keep you from completely abandoning yourself to Jesus. His love is better than life. Get into a quiet place and have a heart-to-heart talk with Him. Pour out your heart to Him. Let His love overshadow you and love you back to life.

Carried along by My Father

Psalm 84: 1 & 2
*How lovely is Your tabernacle, O Lord of hosts! My soul
longs, yes even faints for the courts of the Lord;
my heart and my flesh cry out for the living God.*

When others were overwhelmed by my circumstances and
they could not understand how I was functioning, I
directed them to the love of My Father. For His love has
taken me into the sphere of angels. His love has taken me
to places unseen in the natural. I am carried along by a
love this world knows not of. The cost to enter into His
sacrificial love is high. It cost Jesus His life. I will give Him
no less, extravagant worship. His love not only sustains me
but it satisfies me.

**Lord, Your love has captured my heart and revived my
soul. You have healed my brokenness and set me free to
love. Your love is the wind in my step, the air in my
breath; it's the warmth surrounding me. Your love has
put a fire within that cannot be quenched or stopped.
Your love is healing, restoring and unending. It is forever
mine. When I doubt who I am or how far I've come, I
remember Your love and how You have saved, restored,
delivered and healed me. You are the flame of fire on my
heart. I live to burn for You. Forever we will be, lovers
throughout eternity.**

Reflection:

Silence the noise in your life. Still the many voices telling
you what you should do in your situation. Though people
mean well, it is vital you hear from the Spirit of God

yourself. Give Him all your cares. Then worship Him with an abandoned heart. Don't hold anything back. He will move heaven and earth to rescue you. He will lavish you with His love and do for you what you nor anyone else could ever do.

The Heart of The Father To His Beloved Bride

Song of Songs 4:10
How Much Better Than Wine is Your Love

Beloved, there is nothing I cherish more than to know your heart is Mine. I have loved you with an unending love and have wrapped My love around you securely. I have carried you along and you have found great delight in Me. You are My cherished one and My love for you is unending. Continue to dwell with Me, My love, stay in My presence, for I will never let you go. You will always have your place of honor with Me.

I know your heart's cry; I see what you have been through. I have raised you up and placed you high above your trials. You have glorified Me through it all. Your example has taught others how to run to the Father in the midst of great trials. I am faithful to my covenant of love, for I am a covenant keeping God. Nothing can compare with My love, for I am the God of love.

CATHY COPPOLA

ABOUT THE AUTHOR

Cathy Coppola is a lover of God's presence and a full time minister of the gospel. She has a mandate from God, to preach the word of God and signs and wonders follow.

She has been married to her husband, Phil, for 28 years and together they have raised their four children.

She is a conference speaker, the administrator for Elevated to Excellence and founder of "Where the Fire Meets the Clouds Ministry"; a ministry of healing and setting captives free.

Walking in the supernatural is part of her everyday life. Yielded to the Spirit of God, she ministers healing, deliverance and salvation to broken lives and sees them restored to God's original design.

Her passion is to release the Kingdom of God everywhere she goes.

CATHY COPPOLA

MINISTRY CONTACT INFORMATION

CATHY COPPOLA INTERNATIONAL MINISTRIES

PO BOX 2923

MISSION VIEJO, CA 92690

WEBSITE ADDRESS:

WWW.CATHYCOPPOLA.COM

EMAIL ADDRESS:

CATHYCOPPOLA@GMAIL.COM

Made in the USA
San Bernardino, CA
30 May 2014